Blackpool's Seaside Herita

Blackpool's Seaside Heritage

Allan Brodie and Matthew Whitfield

ENGLISH HERITAGE

Front cover
In recent years Blackpool's seafront has been widened, new trams have been created and giant dune grass sculptures sway in the wind. The iconic Tower is in the middle of a lengthy restoration programme.
[DP154540]

Inside front cover
They Shoot Horses Don't They?, the world's largest mirrorball, was designed by the artist Michael Trainor and was placed on the new sea defences near the Pleasure Beach in 2002.
[AA053279]

Acknowledgements page
Detail from panelling in refreshment room in the Opera House at the Winter Gardens.
[DP117396]

Frontispiece
Blackpool's beach has disappeared at high tide, but crowds still gather on the sloping sea defences. This photograph was taken between the completion of the Tower in 1894 and the erection of the Giant Wheel at the Winter Gardens in 1896.
[BB88/00109]

Back cover
This recipe for a Blackpool breakfast is one of the hundreds of jokes that make up part of the Comedy Carpet in front of Blackpool Tower.
[DP140680]

Published by English Heritage, The Engine House, Fire Fly Avenue, Swindon SN2 2EH
www.english-heritage.org.uk
English Heritage is the Government's statutory adviser on all aspects of the historic environment.

© English Heritage 2014

Images (except as otherwise shown) © English Heritage or © Crown copyright. EH.

Figs 12 and 42 are © and database right Crown Copyright and Landmark Information Group Ltd (All rights reserved 2014). Licence numbers 00394 and TP0024.

First published 2014

ISBN 978-1-84802-110-5
Product code 51673

British Library Cataloguing in Publication Data
A CIP catalogue record for this book is available from the British Library.

For more information about images from the English Heritage Archive contact the Archive Services Team, the Engine House, Fire Fly Avenue, Swindon SN2 2EH; telephone (01793) 414600.

Brought to publication by Sarah Enticknap, Publishing, English Heritage.
Edited by John King.
Page layout by Andrea Rollinson, Ledgard Jepson Ltd.
Printed in the UK by Park Communications Ltd.

Contents

Acknowledgements

This study of Blackpool's architectural development has relied on assistance from a wide range of people. Carl Carrington, the Built Heritage Manager of Blackpool Council, and Jan Cresswell, Heritage Assets Officer, have provided invaluable information and advice on Blackpool's heritage. Blackpool's Central Library contains an unrivalled collection of material about the town's history, and Tony Sharkey and his team in the Local and Family History Centre supplied vast amounts of important research material and advice. Ted and Anne Lightbown have generously shared their detailed knowledge of Blackpool's history and commented on the manuscript. Kathryn Sather, who has written Conservation Management Plans on the Winter Gardens and Tower, has kindly provided copies of her informative reports, and Kate Shane and her staff at Blackpool Tower have given their time generously.

Informed advice and assistance have been provided by a number of colleagues in English Heritage including Henry Owen-John and Darren Ratcliffe in English Heritage's North West Office and Barry Jones, who have read and commented on the manuscript. Peter Williams, Steve Cole, Bob Skingle and James O Davies have taken excellent photographs for this book between 2002 and 2012, and Philip Sinton produced the maps for this book. Steve Ridgeway of ridgewaydesign. com prepared the development drawing of the Winter Gardens and Katy Whitaker has helped with obtaining aerial photographs from the Aerofilms Collection.

Foreword

Since the middle of the 18th century, Blackpool has been attracting visitors, initially to bathe in the sea to improve their health, but by the end of the 19th century the town was synonymous with fun. Its miles of golden sands were crowded with families relaxing in deckchairs and children riding on donkeys. Its Winter Gardens, the Grand Theatre, three piers, the thrilling rides of the Pleasure Beach and the Tower are still popular with millions of visitors each year. Its seafront has been plied by trams for over 125 years and for two months each year the seafront becomes the glittering home to Blackpool's famous illuminations. To accommodate its visitors, streets of lodgings and boarding houses developed near Blackpool's main stations, and large hotels were erected to the north and south of the rapidly growing town in the late 19th and early 20th centuries.

By the end of the 20th century many seaside resorts were experiencing a decline in popularity. In addition, Blackpool was suffering from significant social problems and was also under threat from the sea, the central part of its seafront requiring rapid and major reconstruction. In 2003, a Masterplan was published, plotting how Blackpool would be regenerated through work on a number of its distinctive neighbourhoods, and a key part of the plan was to construct new sea defences. Included in this major project has been the creation of a series of large headlands projecting seawards to provide performance areas, as well as four 30m-high dune grass sculptures that sway gently in the wind. The project also includes, in front of the Tower, the Comedy Carpet, a homage to British humour.

Fun is at the heart of this regeneration project and Blackpool is very conscious of its unrivalled heritage of entertainment. In 2010 the local authority purchased the Winter Gardens and the Tower, and has embarked on refurbishment programmes to ensure that these world-class venues will continue to bring a smile to everyone's face. English Heritage has actively supported these programmes and has assisted with other initiatives to make the town's colourful past play a key role in its bright future.

Sir Laurie Magnus
Chair of English Heritage

1

Introduction

In 1919 Thomas Luke celebrated Blackpool as 'one of the wonders of the world' and 15 years later J B Priestley proclaimed it to be 'the great roaring spangled beast'.[1] Both were alluding to the scale, colour and lights of Britain's most popular resort, which provided visitors with entertainment and accommodation on an industrial scale. The Winter Gardens and the Tower offered holidaymakers opulence for sixpence, relying for their success on the millions of visitors who arrived each year, and Blackpool's three piers and the rides at the Pleasure Beach were further evidence that the technologies that had transformed industry were providing visitors with new, thrilling pleasures. At its height Blackpool could boast more than 10 million visitors per year and in the 1930s its entertainment venues could seat more than 60,000 people each night.

The reason for Blackpool's initial development was an interest in sea bathing, which had started to become popular in England during the second quarter of the 18th century. At Blackpool it is first recorded in the 1750s and by the 1780s a handful of its largest houses were accommodating the village's wealthy visitors. By the early 19th century the first small, purpose-built facilities were being established, catering for a middle-class market, though some writers were already observing that substantial numbers of working people from manufacturing towns were being drawn to Blackpool's charms.

Blackpool remained a small settlement through the early years of the 19th century. In 1801 fewer than 500 people lived there; in 1851 this had risen just over five-fold, but the arrival of the railway in 1846 was the essential development that would eventually transport millions of visitors each year. The half-century following the opening of the first pier in 1863 saw the construction of two further piers, the Winter Gardens, Blackpool Tower and the earliest surviving rides at Blackpool Pleasure Beach (Fig 1). Huge swathes of housing were built for Blackpool's rapidly growing population, which had surpassed 50,000 by the beginning of the 20th century. On the seafront and in distinctive areas near the railway stations, much of the housing stock served as lodgings and boarding houses. Although working-class tourists dominated the heart of the resort during the summer months, Blackpool still catered for a significant middle-class market during spring and autumn, and in residential areas such as North Shore they could remain aloof from the lively centre of the resort.

In 1920 an aeroplane from the recently established Aerofilms flew past Blackpool Tower, which was emblazoned with the sign 'The Wonderland of the World'. The Great Wheel of the Winter Gardens is visible behind. [EPW002080]

Figure 1
Central Pier, the second of Blackpool's piers, opened in 1868. It was located near the newly opened Central Station and proved popular with visitors and excursionists as a venue for dancing, an activity that would have been frowned upon at the North Pier. [AA058348]

Blackpool remained a popular destination throughout much of the 20th century. Buses and cars gradually replaced the train as the main means of reaching the resort and electricity brought the illuminations, colourful rides at the Pleasure Beach, cinemas and its much-loved trams. In contrast to most resorts Blackpool increased in size during World War II as it remained open while towns nearer the continent were closed, and many civil servants and military personnel were sent to live and work in the town.

After the war Blackpool remained Britain's busiest resort but, as the economy grew, people were able to afford holidays abroad and found other types of leisure activities. Many resorts were increasingly perceived to be old-fashioned and even scruffy, and Blackpool's negative image may explain why the number of holidaymakers had decreased, though millions were still visiting each year. The town's declining population suffered from high rates of unemployment, low wages and problematic levels of ill health and crime; its building stock was in a poor condition, which was exacerbated by a contraction in the quantity of holiday accommodation required.

Figure 2
The Comedy Carpet in front of Blackpool Tower pays homage to more than a thousand comedians and comic writers. It is the centrepiece of the Tower Festival Headland, where concerts can be staged. One of the new trams can be seen running past the Tower.
[DP157272]

To deal with these problems Blackpool is implementing a Masterplan, published in 2003, to regenerate the town's distinctive neighbourhoods, its town centre and its seafront. Major investment has created new sea defences, a modern tram system and a new public realm including the popular Comedy Carpet (Fig 2) and four 30m-high dune grass sculptures that sway gently in the wind.

Blackpool's distinctive heritage is playing a significant role in the regeneration of the town. In 1969 Nikolaus Pevsner noted with surprise that Blackpool had no listed buildings, and it was one of the last local authorities to designate any conservation areas. However, over the past four decades 41 structures and buildings have been designated, and Stanley Park and part of the town centre have become Conservation Areas. A Townscape Heritage Initiative was launched in April 2006 with £2.3 million of public funding to stimulate private investment in the town centre, and during the subsequent six years many buildings were refurbished. Alongside this programme Blackpool Council has been investing in improving the public realm, and in 2012 work began on the creation of the Talbot Gateway development to create new homes and a central business district near Blackpool North Station. Not all parts of the Masterplan have been delivered. The former Central Station site was to be the location for a new Regional Casino with accompanying hotels, but Manchester rather than Blackpool was chosen to be its site in 2007. Subsequently, the concept of casino-led regeneration fell out of favour and was abandoned.

In 2006 Blackpool caused considerable merriment in the media with its announcement that it would seek to be designated a World Heritage Site, a mirth heightened by contrasting its boarding houses and Blackpool Tower with the Pyramids and the Great Barrier Reef. This audacious proposal noted that Blackpool had 'Outstanding Universal Value' as the world's first working-class seaside resort, an identity that it has retained despite a reduction in its visitor numbers. Blackpool was not included on the United Kingdom's 2011 tentative list for World Heritage status, not through a lack of historical significance but as a result of the limited survival of the physical fabric that illuminates this history. Its bid for this accolade would, however, have found favour with Thomas Luke and the owners of the Tower who a century earlier had proclaimed it to be 'The Wonderland of the World'.

2 The origins of Blackpool

Early Blackpool 1750–1840

Blackpool is located at the west side of the Fylde, a wide plain of agricultural farmland described in 1841 as 'flat and indifferently-cultivated land'.[2] Before the 19th century, it was sparsely populated, with small villages at Bispham and Poulton-le-Fylde and a scatter of smaller hamlets including Layton, Great Marton and Little Marton. There was no harbour and little commercial activity apart from farming and some handloom weaving, and the poor state of the roads provided considerable challenges to potential visitors.

An oral tradition, apparently first recorded in 1837 by Revd Thornber, recounts how Ethart-a-Whiteside had opened the first facility for visitors almost a century earlier because his Welsh wife was an accomplished cook. The earliest contemporary reference to sea-bathing visitors occurs in June 1754 when Bishop Richard Pococke recorded tersely that 'At Blackpool, near the sea, are accommodations for people who come to bathe.'[3] In 1788 William Hutton said that the only place where visitors could stay 40 years earlier was the Foxhall, and in 1824 Edward Baines claimed that Blackpool as 'a place of fashionable resort for the recovery of health is not of more than seventy years standing', again suggesting a mid-18th-century origin.[4]

From the early 18th century documents begin to refer to people venturing into the sea in England wherever there was convenient access. By the 1730s facilities for visitors were being provided at Scarborough, Liverpool, Margate and Brighton and within a few decades more than a dozen towns were welcoming sea bathers. Visitors were attracted to these settlements because they offered accommodation and at least rudimentary bathing facilities and entertainments. It was only in the late 18th and early 19th centuries that new settlements began to develop for bathers on previously undeveloped stretches of coast, such as at Bognor Regis, Southport and Weston-super-Mare. Therefore, Blackpool's origin as a sea-bathing location in the 1750s means that it predated by decades other new resorts established on a largely undeveloped coastline, though its growth remained slow until the 19th century.

William Bartlett's drawing of 1840, engraved by Edward Finden and published in 1842, shows the largest seafront houses, including Bailey's Hotel at the left-hand side.

Blackpool in the late 18th century

The earliest detailed descriptions of Blackpool were written by William Hutton
(1723–1815), a self-made businessman, writer and historian, and his daughter
Catherine (1756–1846), who had visited the village in August and October
1788. Coming from Birmingham, the Huttons were unusual visitors, the
majority of whom came from the growing urban populations of Lancashire
and the West Riding of Yorkshire. In 1781 stagecoach services began to run
during the summer from inland Lancashire and the West Riding and in 1783
accommodation for bathing was advertised in Manchester. Catherine Hutton
characterised Blackpool's visitors in terms of the better company, which
consisted of 'Lancashire gentry, Liverpool merchants, and Manchester
manufacturers' as well as the more lowly 'species called Boltoners' which she
described as 'rich, rough manufacturers'.[5] A visitor from Halifax at the end
of the 18th century described Blackpool as a 'healthy spot' that 'derives its
chief support from Preston, Blackburn, Manchester, Wigan, and Bolton; and
immense quantities of people resort here from Leeds and other parts of
Yorkshire'. The Yorkshire House was described as 'a kind of lodging-house
for people from Halifax'.[6]

    The Huttons found that Blackpool attracted a broad cross-section of the
population. William noted that during the 1760s visitors had been 'chiefly of
the lower class' and in 1788 he recorded the presence of 'the inferior class
whose sole motive for visiting this airy region, is health'.[7] Richard Ayton, who
passed through Blackpool in 1813, recorded that 'Among the company are
crowds of poor people from the manufacturing towns, who have a high opinion
of the efficacy of bathing, maintaining that in the months of August and
September there is physic in the sea'.[8] The presence of a significant number
of people of the 'inferior class' marked Blackpool out from other resorts. For
instance, Margate was attracting London tradesmen as early as the 1770s
because they could reach the resort on sailing boats along the Thames.
However, it was not until steamers appeared in 1815, and especially after the
arrival of the railway in 1846, that Margate gained significant numbers of
working-class visitors.

    Wealthy visitors travelled to Blackpool by coach, but others might travel
more cheaply by cart, though Ayton believed that some of the hardiest had

made it on foot from Manchester. They apparently came for three or four days and paid 9d a day for lodgings, which involved five or six beds 'crammed into each room, and five or six people into each bed'.[9] Revd Thornber provided a similar account of working-class visitors fleeing from their 'confined, filthy, smoky' towns to bathe and drink seawater during the warmest summer days. In 1827 an influx of visitors from Blackburn, Burnley, Colne, Padiham and the borders of Yorkshire arrived in carts and they were nicknamed 'padjamers' because of the colour of their stockings. To be accommodated some slept four to a bed in shifts and 'out-houses and barns were in high request', though perhaps the most unlucky had to sleep in coaches or in bathing machines.[10] The prominence of lower-class visitors in contemporary accounts is probably because their presence was noteworthy, but this should not disguise the fact that Blackpool's early visitors were broadly middle class.

Blackpool in 1788 consisted of a scatter of about fifty houses, with six of the largest being used as the principal accommodation for visitors. In August 1788 Catherine Hutton stayed at 'the house of 80, which is called the Lane's End', though there was another house capable of housing 100 visitors, figures achieved, according to Richard Ayton, by 'a system of packing'.[11] From north to south along the seafront the houses were known as Bailey's Hotel (on the site of the Metropole), Forshaw's Hotel (where the Clifton Hotel now stands), Hudson's Hotel (Lane's End according to Catherine Hutton), Hull's Hotel (later the Royal Hotel), the Yorkshire House and Foxhall. Accommodation was also provided at Bonny's-in-the-Fields, which was located near where the King Edward VII Hotel would later be constructed, and at the Gynn, to the north of the village.

In 1792 John Hudson placed an advertisement in which he described how he had prepared his house in Blackpool for visitors:

> JOHN HUDSON at the Centre House, returns his grateful Thanks to his Friends for the Favours they have been pleased to confer on him, and hopes they will continue the same, as nothing will be wanted in his Power to render the Accommodations agreeable. He has this Season fitted up his House, in the genteelest Manner, for the Reception of the first Families. Private Parlours to let, together with one fronting the Sea, with a large Bow-window.

Also a Suite of Rooms to let to a large Family, or Party, consisting of a Dining Room twelve Yards by seven, a Drawing Room over it, both which have Bow-windows, containing eleven best Beds, and as many Servants' Beds as may be required.[12]

The form of some of the seafront buildings is known from engravings and early photographs. Bailey's Hotel, one of the houses in existence by the 1780s, was a substantial three-storeyed Georgian house with a large cross wing lit by a semi-circular bow window (Fig 3). Photographs of the Clifton Arms Hotel taken before the mid-1870s show the early part of the building that was Forshaw's Hotel. Like nearby Bailey's it was a substantial, three-storeyed Georgian building and had a pair of three-storeyed bay windows facing the sea (Fig 4). After the Restoration, Edward Tyldesley built Foxhall, 'a small sequestered residence as a summer retreat' surrounded by a high wall of cobble stones, and although the house was only a modest-sized structure, it was considered 'a stately mansion' in comparison with the 'few clay-built and rush-roofed huts'[13] (Fig 5). Each of its two floors apparently contained four or five rooms and one wing was used as a chapel, which survived longer than the rest of the house.

Figure 5
This view of some of the buildings at Foxhall shows that it may have had a hall range with a cross wing with an inline, thatched barn or shippon. The house was lit by a mixture of 17th-century mullioned-and-transomed windows and some 18th-century sashes.
[From Blackpool's Progress 1926]

As well as the handful of large houses there were smaller dwellings, the homes of local farmers and fishermen. In 1788 William Hutton said that Foxhall 'must have stood, the little hall among huts' and a year later Samuel Finney III noted that 'there are 6 or 7 large handsome houses for the Reception of Company interspersed with small Inclosures and neat Fishermens Huts'.[14] In 1837 Revd Thornber described the 'huts' as 'composed chiefly of wattles and clay, together with about a dozen houses of superior make and pretension, built on crooks'.[15] As late as 1835 the vicarage at Poulton-le-Fylde was still 'a thatched building of two stories, the upper one open to the roof and supported on crooks', with a later cross wing.[16] These writers were describing the vernacular tradition of the Fylde, the homes of fishermen, small farmers or weavers. These houses were small, cruck-built, thatched, single- or one-and-a-half- storeyed buildings, some of which were longhouses combining domestic accommodation with a shippon. A description of the opening of Blackpool's first pier in 1863 recorded that 'in a few odd corners' there were still 'traces of the low, mud built, thatched dwellings which were the temporary homes of visitors to the place during even modern memory'.[17] Fumbler's Hill Cottages, which lay to the north of where the Metropole stands, survived to the end of the 19th century. They faced southwards rather than looking out to sea and are the cottages depicted in the 1842 engraving (Fig 6). The external walls of these vernacular buildings might be constructed of 'clam staff and daub' in which clay was applied to thin vertical timbers, or cob, which required thicker walls. To avoid damp, the mud walling stood on a foundation layer of cobble stones. Today, no examples of these types of houses seem to exist within the modern boundaries of Blackpool, though photographs show a number surviving through the 19th century.

In 1836 Edward Baines claimed that 'The houses are chiefly built of sea-stone, a hard and fragile substance', and a number of vernacular houses with external walls constructed of beach stones survive (Figs 7 and 8).[18] As Revd Thornber observed, early houses in the Fylde employed crucks, and a number of examples have been recorded. Ivy Cottage at Bispham was unusual as it had a painted date of 1686 on a panel in the hall, though it is uncertain whether this commemorated the construction of the house or the insertion of the hearth. It consisted of four full crucks and its lobby-entry plan contained a kitchen and a hall with a small parlour and buttery opening off it.

Most of these modest dwellings probably survived from the 17th century, but it was local, often poor-quality brick that became a new medium for the

Figure 6
This detail from the 1842 engraving shows the roofs of the small, thatched buildings that still existed near the heart of the resort beyond Bailey's Hotel, where the Metropole would later be built.

Figure 7
1–2 Fisher Lane is an attractive pair of small, rural cottages that has a recently renewed thatched roof. [DP154958]

Figure 8
239 Layton Road at Layton is a rare survivor from one of the small inland hamlets. Its main façade shows clearly the beach stone that has been used in its construction. [DP154959]

belated 'Great Rebuilding' in the Fylde that peaked during the first quarter of the 18th century. The new material led to the appearance of two- and two-and-a-half-storeyed houses with lobby-entry and double-pile plans in place of the previous linear forms. Cross wings, which first appeared in the second half of the 17th century, became more common. Thatch continued as a roofing material, but increasingly thin stone flags or slate were also employed, though Baines in 1836 only recorded four houses with slate roofs in Blackpool. Despite the appearance of brick, cobble remained popular and Walker's Hill Farmhouse on Midgeland Road, the best surviving example of the enlarged and more sophisticated vernacular house, employs cobble stone for its external walling.

A growing number of vernacular buildings from the late 18th and early 19th centuries are known from photographs, and a handful of restored examples have survived within Blackpool. They share the same wide, low, two- and occasionally three-storeyed form. For instance, the main block of the Gynn Inn was three-storeyed with a two-storeyed extension to one side, and both parts seem to have had slate roofs. It closed in May 1921 and was demolished soon after. The earlier part of Bonny's-in-the-Fields, one of Blackpool's earliest lodging houses, consisted of a two-storeyed row of three houses with a slate roof, and by 1787 a three-storeyed, two-bay extension had been added to the end of the terrace (Fig 9). The Saddle Inn on Whitegate Drive is a low, wide, two-storeyed building, apparently of the late 18th century, and a short distance

Figure 9
This old photograph of Bonny's-in-the-Fields, taken shortly before its demolition, shows the wide, low form of the buildings. The later extension is on the left-hand side of the photograph.
[From Blackpool's Progress *1926]*

Figure 10
Raikes Hall originally had large gardens, which became a pleasure ground in the 1870s. Today only the house with its attached bowling green survives.
[DP157218]

to the north the No. 3 pub has a similar form. The Bull Hotel on Waterloo Road in South Shore shows that this simple form persisted into the second quarter of the 19th century, and the original Star Inn, beside where the Pleasure Beach evolved, and the Cottage on Newhouse Road, Marton, appear to be among the latest known examples as they do not appear on the Ordnance Survey map of the mid-1840s.

All these buildings were vernacular in style and modest in size. The only surviving Georgian building of some architectural distinction within Blackpool is Raikes Hall, a kilometre from the seafront, east of the emerging village (Fig 10). This five-bay, three-storeyed, stuccoed, brick house of the mid-18th century was built in c 1760 by William Boucher and an advertisement for a lease described its layout in 1787. The ground floor contained three parlours, a servants' hall, a butler's pantry and the kitchen. Each of the two upper floors had four lodging rooms and there were also lodging rooms for servants, and gardens, orchards, stables and outbuildings.

As well as providing accommodation for visitors, Blackpool was beginning to develop facilities for bathing and entertainment. By 1788 a well-organised bathing regimen had evolved. People came to bathe during July and August and ideally this took place at high tide, when the sea was closer to the shore. William Hutton described the procedure for sea bathing:

> A bell rings at the time of bathing, as a signal for the ladies. Some use machines drawn by one horse, a few travel from their apartments in their waterdress, but the majority clothe in the boxes, which stand on the beach for their use. If a gentleman is seen upon the parade he forfeits a bottle of wine. When the ladies retire, the bell rings for the gentlemen, who act a second part in the same scene.[19]

Bathing machines had been in use at other resorts since at least the 1730s, and where there was only a short length of beach men and women would bathe at separate times. What is surprising is that this occurred at Blackpool with its long beach; Brighton, with a similar length of shoreline, enforced separate areas for male and female bathers. Also surprising is a reference to bathers coming from their apartments ready for the sea, an early reference to what became known as 'Macintosh bathing', a practice that was frowned upon until the early 20th century.

Blackpool's concentration of accommodation in a handful of large houses meant that much of the socialising took place within these semi-closed communities, which William Hutton likened to 'a private family, or a kingdom'.[20] In 1789 Samuel Finney III described 'Eating, Drinking and Conversation' in his hotel, though other houses offered 'card playing, and sometimes Balls'.[21] William Hutton recounted how in the 1760s the only place of 'public resort' was 'that little white cottage at the lane end, now the news house', while the current 'coffee-room' was still a blacksmith's shop.[22] A shop opened in 1789 and in the same year a subscription was launched to provide a church, though the building only opened in 1821. Acts of worship were previously conducted in 'unconsecrated temples', rooms attached to one of the large houses, otherwise visitors faced a long walk to the parish church in Bispham.[23] Visitors could also enjoy Blackpool's first promenade – 6yd (5m) wide and 200yd (183m) long – a 'pretty grass-walk on the verge of the sea bank' separated from the road by white rails (Fig 11).[24] There were also bowling greens (though Hutton decried them as 'diminutive'), there were boats for sailing out to sea and butts had been set up for archery. In 1788 the theatre was still an agricultural building, Hutton noting that 'during nine months in the year is only the threshing floor of a barn'. Hutton described how 'Rows of benches are placed one behind another, and honoured with the names of *pit* and *gallery*, the first, two shillings the other one [*sic*]. The house is said to hold six pounds; it was half filled.'[25]

Figure 11
This view in 1840 shows the large houses overlooking the small promenade that ran along the friable cliffs, which would soon require consolidation.

The picture that emerges from William Hutton's description is of limited facilities for visitors in buildings adapted to serve as places of 'public resort'. With only 400 visitors at the peak of its season, no investor would be willing to spend money on purpose-built facilities in this still modest-sized village. With the exception of Scarborough, which already had entertainments for its spa visitors, all the main 18th-century resorts went through this phase of adapting existing buildings before the numbers of visitors and, perhaps as importantly, the guarantee of their return each year meant that a significant amount of money could be risked with some certainty of a return.

Blackpool before the railway

The earliest comprehensive description of Blackpool records the town in 1816, but it is an account of a conversation with an elderly resident that was first published 60 years later. Nevertheless, comparison with other sources, including an 1818 map and a description of 1821, suggests that it is broadly accurate. In 1816 the large houses used as hotels were the main feature of the seafront and the description includes mentions of a number of thatched cottages. Along Church Street there were already a number of cottages with slate roofs and in 1817 Blackpool's first school was built further inland along what was still the village's only significant street. In 1821 the opening of Blackpool's long-awaited church cemented Church Street's central role in the subsequent development of the town (Fig 12). The evidence of the 1838 tithe map, the first edition of the Ordnance Survey map and the census figures suggests that the settlement was only growing slowly. The population of Layton with Warbreck, which included Blackpool, increased from 473 in 1801 to 943 in 1831 and to 1,968 in 1841. However, as the last two censuses were enumerated in late May and early June, they would have included more visitors than in 1801 and 1851 when the censuses were conducted in March. Revd Thornber reported that in 1836 'Great improvements were made in the appearance of the village; shops beautified and increased in number, cottages ornamented and built upon a more modern construction, and, at a moderate calculation, we may affirm that 200 beds were added to the other accommodations of the village.'[26] Thornber still referred to Blackpool as a

Figure 12
This Ordnance Survey map, surveyed in 1844 and published in 1847, shows the small size of Blackpool when the railway arrived. Church Street was the central axis of the settlement, though Talbot Road from the station to the beach is depicted. Although apparently compiled in the 1840s, the railway into Central Station, which opened in 1863, had been added to the map.

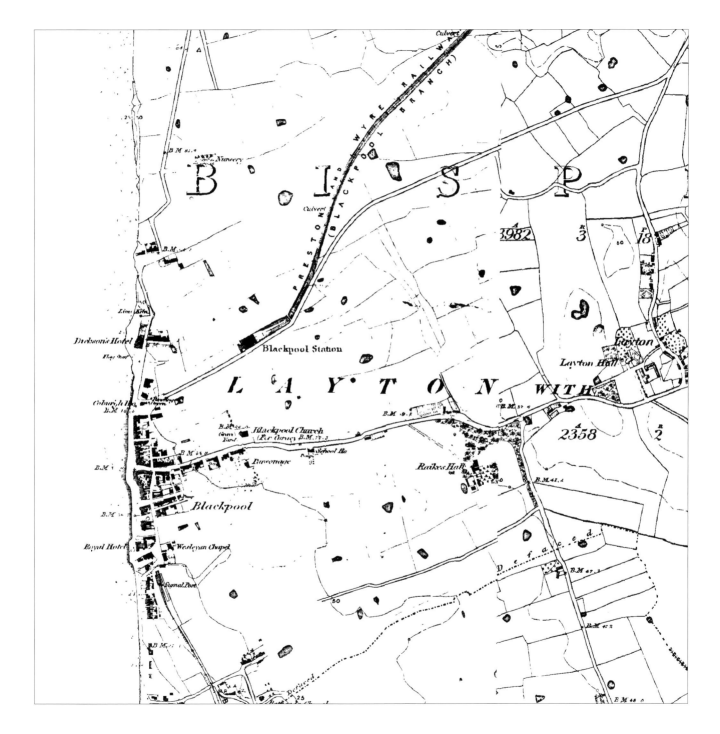

village, and the 1838 tithe map suggests it was still a modest-sized and fairly dispersed settlement focused on the seafront and on either side of Church Street, with a smaller area of development a short distance to the south at the Yorkshire House and Foxhall.

By 1838 a new, small settlement was developing further to the south, named Southshore or South Shore. Until the 18th century this area, known as Layton Hawes, was an area of common land with sandy soil and poor drainage. In 1767 a number of the leading freeholders petitioned for an Act of Parliament to enclose this area, creating a grid of major roads and lanes, flanked by drainage ditches that enclosed large areas of land that were subdivided into fields. The main roads of South Shore and the pattern of development in the 19th century would follow the geographical framework established in the late 1760s. The first house was apparently built by Thomas Moore in 1819, and in the late 1820s it supposedly remained the sole house there, though the 1818 map shows a number of pre-existing, probably small agricultural structures. In 1841 A B Granville enthused about the 'new colony of visiters and bathers' that was growing, and some vestiges of this early settlement have survived (Fig 13).[27] Using the 1838 tithe map, and assuming that South Shore followed Blackpool's example, the small two-storeyed houses in the street behind the seafront may have been accompanied by taller, grander houses on the seafront, but none of these has survived.

The accommodation arrangements in Blackpool described by Revd Thornber in 1837 were still broadly the same as in the late 1780s, though the buildings seem to have been significantly updated in the intervening decades. Finden's two engravings of Blackpool, prepared in 1840 and published in 1842, show that three-storeyed houses with three-storeyed, polygonal bay windows were appearing on the seafront, but these became more widespread during the ensuing decades (*see* Chapter 2 opening image and Fig 11). The most distinguished new house on the seafront was West Hey, which was built in 1837 by the Manchester banker Sir Benjamin Heywood as his summer residence (Fig 14).

The hotels were the most expensive places to stay, costing from 2s 6d to 7s per day according to the time of year, the quality of the room being let and the status of the hotel. Blackpool also seems to have had a number of lodging houses, houses in which guests would rent rooms and purchase their own

Figure 13
A small, two-storeyed house on Bolton Street has a date
of 1835 on a window sill, but this is partly painted and
cannot be used with certainty, though it is in a row
of small houses that appear on the 1838 tithe map.
[AA053081]

ingredients and their hosts would prepare their meals. Visitors could also rent rooms in cottages, ranging from three to a dozen beds, rather than bedrooms. These could be rented for 1s a day per room and, although Revd Thornber praised their comforts, they were likely to be more basic than the larger hotels. In 1831 Peter Wittle wrote: 'Several handsome cottages have been erected, many of which are built in the neat cottage orneé style, (many would call them gothic,) which gives them a neat and elegant appearance'.[28] It seems that Blackpool's architecture had come full circle from the thatched vernacular cottages of the Fylde to the polite cottage ornée.

Blackpool seems to have differed from many early resorts because of the concentration of entertainment within the hotels. In the 1830s assemblies were still being held in large rooms in the hotels, but by 1840 a number of independent entertainment venues had emerged. In 1821 there was a 'Coffee-

room, News-room, and Library' and in 1837 'Carter's News-room' was in Church Street.[29] Billiard tables were provided by the postmaster, George Cooke, at the north corner of Church Street and the promenade, but as late as the 1850s any theatrical productions still had to rely on the use of an adapted agricultural building beside an inn. Visitors could use baths at a number of locations, including at most of the hotels, and an early photograph of the County and Lane Ends Hotel after it was rebuilt in the mid-1860s shows part of the bathhouse that had been built in 1837. This was a modest, two-storeyed structure only recognisable as a bathhouse by a large sign over its front door. According to the 1838 tithe map William Bonny also ran a bathing house where Chapel Street met the seafront, near the site of the Trocadero.

Figure 14
Sir Benjamin Heywood's house was a substantial, three-storeyed, brick building with a polygonal bay window facing the sea. After his death it was converted into an aquarium. It was on the site of the southern end of Blackpool Tower.
[From Blackpool's Progress *1926*]

Figure 15
This photograph of the Victoria Terrace and
Promenade was taken in the 1860s when it was
called the Crystal Palace. It shows a long terrace
of shops with large display windows, with the
long room above with French windows opening
onto a wide, south-facing balcony.
[From Blackpool's Progress 1926]

These independent facilities seem to have been very modest until the late 1830s when the Victoria Terrace and Promenade was built at the corner of Victoria Street and Bank Hey Street (Fig 15). Opened in May 1837, it was built by Dr John Cocker to provide a 'fashionable lounge' with an 'attached news-room, billiard table, and library'.[30] It consisted of 'seven handsome shops' with a 32yd (29m) -long room, 'designed in an airy and graceful style of architecture' with 'its folding windows upon a balcony six feet wide'. The 'graceful style' of the building involved employing Doric columns to support the balcony and the porch at the end of the building, while the upper storey was divided by simple, undecorated pilasters. For a town later celebrated for its carnivalesque architecture, this was an essay in restraint, its 'chaste' exterior apparently being in contrast to its 'spacious and magnificent' saloon.[31] It

Figure 16
This photograph of St John's Church was taken shortly
before its tower was replaced in 1866. It reveals
how the small original structure was enlarged in
a piecemeal fashion during the mid-19th century.
[From Blackpool's Progress *1926]*

survived until the end of the 20th century, when it was replaced by modern retail units that were completed in 2000.

Private investors like Dr Cocker were behind the creation of new entertainment facilities, but the provision of a church, an essential feature for any aspiring resort, required investment by the wider community (Fig 16). A subscription was launched in 1789, but the first meeting to arrange the construction of the building only took place in 1818. The church, which was consecrated in July 1821, cost £1,072 and of this £800 was contributed by ten of Blackpool's leading citizens. The church was enlarged in 1832–3, but was still too small to accommodate the increasing population, and there were further plans in the mid-1830s to extend it, though this only occurred a decade later. For Nonconformists an Independent Chapel opened in 1825, and a Romanesque-style Wesleyan Chapel opened in Bank Hey Street a decade later to house up to 300 worshippers.

Despite the improved facilities being provided in the 1820s and 1830s the key reason for visiting Blackpool remained its natural qualities. As well as sea bathing, visitors used the sea for sailing and rowing, and sometimes they were able to board the steam packet running from Liverpool to Ulverston. The beach was also a venue for promenading and the small parade that existed in the 1780s continued to be popular, though coastal erosion had required the reconstruction and realignment of the seafront road in the 1820s. By 1841 Blackpool had its first sea defences: 'Walls of stone have been built in a slanting direction, to keep up this said cliff, and prevent the else inevitable excavation which high water would make' (*see* Fig 11).[32]

At the end of the Georgian period Blackpool was still a village, with modest facilities aimed at a small, middle-class market, though these visitors were often outnumbered by working people coming from the industrial towns of Lancashire and Yorkshire. In the 1840s the railway arrived, but in the subsequent three decades Blackpool was still providing facilities for middle-class customers and its growth was unremarkable. However, by the end of this period it was clear that investors in the growing town were no longer content simply to cater for a small, local market, but were exhibiting ambitions to make Blackpool a major national resort.

3   The development of the town

The arrival of the railway 1840–1870

In 1840 the Preston and Wyre Railway line to Fleetwood included a station at Poulton-le-Fylde, where visitors could disembark and continue to Blackpool by road. This inconvenient arrangement was short-lived, as Blackpool's first railway station opened in April 1846. The Talbot Road Station was designed by Mr Rampling of Fleetwood and was in marked contrast to the modern station, which is rather unobtrusive (Fig 17). Contemporary newspaper stories reported enthusiastically how new developments were being stimulated by the railway's arrival and a trade directory in 1848 claimed that the railway had led to

> laying out streets and walks – the erection of handsome houses and shops on every side – the establishment of elegant hotels, and billiard, news and coffee rooms, lounges, bazaars &c. – the building of a market place, and the opening and enlargement of places of worship, bespeak the rising importance of the town, and the anxiety of the inhabitants to render the sojourn of their visiters pleasant and comfortable.[33]

This aerial photograph shows Blackpool North Station before the demolition of the older part of the station in the 1970s. It also shows the scale of the platforms needed to deal with the huge numbers of people visiting the resort.
[AFL03/Aerofilms/A223406]

Figure 17 (right)
The original station of 1846, which was located nearer the heart of the emerging town where Talbot Street meets Dickson Road, was probably Blackpool's largest building when it was built. Its main façade was treated with pronounced quoins and a dentil cornice and its large windows were framed by Ionic columns supporting a pediment.
[From Blackpool's Progress *1926]*

However, Blackpool does not seem to have been sufficiently developed in the 1840s to benefit immediately from the arrival of the railway. In 1841 its population numbered just under 2,000, and just over 2,500 in 1851, but by the 1860s Blackpool had shifted from being a village to a small town. In two decades its population doubled to almost 4,000 and key elements of the emerging town's infrastructure were being put in place. To administer Blackpool an Improvement Act was obtained in 1853 specifying the powers of the Local Board of Health (16 Vict c.29). The Board was established for the Township of Layton with Warbreck, the dominance that Blackpool would enjoy in the area not yet being obvious, at least legally. The Board was granted powers to regulate and license a range of activities affecting residents and visitors. Among these were powers to enforce repairs to buildings, to regulate the running of public houses, to erect slaughterhouses, as well as the licensing of bathing machines, pleasure boats, hackney carriages and sedan chairs. It also included sections concerning the running of markets and the provision of gasworks and sea defences.

As well as governmental structure the emerging town needed physical infrastructure. In 1844 St John's Market opened in Market Street at a cost of nearly £1,200. Built in brick and stone in an Elizabethan style, it bore the arms of Thomas Clifton over the north entrance and those of Sir Benjamin Heywood and Revd Thornber over the south. A second market opened in 1861 on South Beach, the stretch of the seafront that would later become known as the Golden Mile. This imposing stone structure, built for William Read, contained 30 stalls for commodities and alongside there was a building containing hot, cold and shower baths, using water drawn from the sea by a steam-powered pump.

Utilities for the growing town were being provided in the 1850s and 1860s. The Vegetable Gas Company's gasworks was erected in 1851–2 at South Beach on Bonny's Estate, and although the Board of Health had the power to purchase this facility, it preferred to build its own coal gas plant. This began to supply gas in September 1853 and by the mid-1860s it had two gasometers. The Board also had powers to improve the sea defences and in 1856 the promenade was repaired and extended. Blackpool's water was supplied by the Fylde Waterworks Company, which was established in 1860. Water began to be pumped in July 1864 and within three years two-thirds of the town's houses were being provided. Dealing with sewage proved a more intractable problem. In 1850 a government inspector found sewage trickling across the beach and draining into the Spen Dyke, the Black Pool that gave the town its name. A scheme to deal with this was completed in 1856–7, using an old watercourse to take sewage southwards where a wood-lined channel took the effluent out to below low-water mark. *The Builder* magazine in 1859 recorded this new arrangement, but noted that new houses were already being built on the shoreline in the vicinity of the outflow, and sewage treatment remained a significant issue until the early 20th century. In 1864, the Royal National Lifeboat Institution established its first lifeboat in a purpose-built station on Lytham Road (Fig 18).

The growing town also required improved places of worship. Despite an enlargement in 1832, the parish church of St John was proving too small and further enlargements occurred in 1847 and in 1851 when the chancel was built

Figure 18
The first lifeboat station building has survived despite the seafront having been extended seawards and the capability and size of lifeboats having increased, necessitating the provision of two later lifeboat stations in 1937 (demolished) and 1998.
[AA058341]

(*see* Fig 16). In 1861 the nave was raised and an arched roof replaced the former, lower, flat ceiling, and in 1866 a larger tower was built. In South Shore the modest Anglican church of the Holy Trinity, which was built in 1836, grew during the next 60 years as its congregation increased. It was enlarged in 1858 when a new transept and chancel capable of seating 380 worshippers were added. The Roman Catholic Church of the Sacred Heart on Talbot Road was designed by Edward Welby Pugin and opened in 1857 at a cost of £5,500. Its nave and aisles date from this period and indicate the scale of the church that was needed to satisfy its residential and seasonal congregation (*see* Fig 69).

A number of other churches were built for various denominations. An Independent Chapel in Victoria Street opened in 1849 in a 'neat Gothic building', while the Union Baptist Chapel in Abingdon Street, which opened in 1861, was a brick building with classical stone detailing.[34] Its site is now occupied by the Post Office. The temporary iron church of Christ Church on Queen Street, which opened in 1861, soon proved too small and was replaced in 1866 (Fig 19). The Wesleyan Chapel of 1835 also proved to be too small and

Figure 19
Christ Church, as rebuilt in 1866, was a large brick-and-pebble church capable of seating 1,000 worshippers in an elaborate Gothic interior. Its site is now occupied by the Jobcentre.
[BB81/05801]

Figure 20
The Talbot Hotel was a modest, two-storeyed structure
with a pebbled façade, gables and gablets with elaborate
bargeboards and mullioned windows. A board announced
the presence of a bowling green behind the hotel.
[From Blackpool's Progress 1926]

in 1862 a new, larger church capable of housing 760 people opened at a cost of £3,500. A United Methodist Free Church in Adelaide Street was founded in 1864, a Temperance Hall was created in Coronation Street in 1867 and the cornerstone of a Wesleyan Chapel in Rawcliffe Street was laid in South Shore in September 1869.

There were also significant improvements to Blackpool's hotels and housing stock. The Talbot Hotel opposite the station was completed by the time the railway arrived (Fig 20). Built by Thomas Clifton in 1845, it would have been dwarfed by the new station. A number of existing hotels on the seafront were extended and south of the main part of the resort the Manchester Hotel was erected in 1845. It resembled a three-storeyed terrace with two-storeyed polygonal bay windows.

In the centre of Blackpool the demolition of Coburg House to the north of the Clifton Arms allowed the creation of Talbot Square at the end of Talbot Road. This would condition where Blackpool's first pier would be erected, at the most direct point on the coast from the railway station. Talbot Road, Clifton Street, Abingdon Street and Birley Street were laid out on land owned by Thomas Clifton and the trustees of the Lytham School. Clifton was seeking to create a prestigious villa development, but instead he chose to invest in Lytham, leaving these streets to more piecemeal development.

Buildings erected in Blackpool between 1840 and 1870 were mostly modest in size and conservative in form. They were two- or three-storeyed and a number of small, apparently early buildings have survived in the town centre. Most potentially early houses are undated and, because of the later removal of architectural detail, are effectively undateable, but in the town centre a small number of dated, pre-1870 buildings survive. On Talbot Road near the Roman Catholic church there is a narrow, three-storeyed building in a short terrace dating from 1857, the year the church was completed (Fig 21). Nearby on

Figure 21
These houses in Talbot Road show the quality and size of some of the best houses being built in Blackpool in the mid-19th century.
[DP154837]

Figure 22
This house in Abingdon Street coincidentally bears the same date as the police station a few metres along the same street, and the façades of both shared a similar overall form, with a large central gable.
[DP154780]

Abingdon Street a two-storeyed building has the date 1862 in its central pediment (Fig 22). Much of this house's detailing has been removed, but in addition to its decorative central pediment it had elaborate corner features. A two-storeyed house in Homer Terrace on the north side of Cedar Square is dated 1865, suggesting the whole of this modest terrace dates from this period. It appears on an 1870 map and this source helps to identify other surviving mid-19th-century buildings (*see* Fig 40). A number of two- and three-storeyed buildings on Talbot Road are survivals from the mid-19th century, and on the east side of Edward Street, near St John's Church, is a two-storeyed terrace with polygonal bay windows. These are not the vernacular buildings that once existed in the heart of Blackpool, but are modest mid-19th-century buildings that have often been heavily reworked.

There were taller buildings on the seafront, as property facing the sea had a higher value as lodgings (Fig 23). In 1840 there were only a handful of three-storeyed buildings with polygonal bay windows, but these became more widespread during the next half-century (*see* Fig 11). In a number of places

Figure 23
A rare seafront survivor from the mid-19th century is the building that had housed Roberts' Oyster Bar since the 19th century. Located at the corner of the Promenade and West Street, beside the Mitre pub, it is three-storeyed and is decorated with simplified, Regency-style 'Ionic' pilasters.
[AA053238]

Figure 24
This is the last remnant of a row of houses on
the seafront between York Street and Yorkshire
Terrace, which probably dates from the 1870s.
[AA058329]

solitary houses with vestiges of bay windows have survived. Albert Terrace, on
the seafront on either side of Queen Square opposite the Metropole, was built
in the 1840s and had three storeys with some two-storeyed bay windows.
One of its original houses is recognisable, though it has lost its ground floor
to a modern shopfront. Further south, near the Central Pier, a pair of three-
storeyed houses survives, the last remnants of a terrace trapped between two
modern entertainment complexes (Fig 24). There were similar large houses
in the central part of Blackpool between the piers, with long front gardens in
which small rides, amusements and stalls gradually accrued for the

entertainment of visitors pouring out of the nearby Central Station, a process that marked their rapid decline in status (Fig 25). These houses proved particularly vulnerable to redevelopment as their wide, long plots were sufficiently large to allow substantial entertainment complexes to be developed during the 20th century. Surviving, comprehensible examples of the standard Victorian housing are rare on the seafront and in central Blackpool, but one old photograph shows a three-storeyed house with two-storeyed, semi-circular bay windows, a common type of fenestration in and around Brighton, but rare in the north-west of England.

The evidence from surviving buildings and early photographs demonstrates that the standard form for larger seafront houses and structures on main streets was a three-storeyed building with two- or three-storeyed

Figure 25
Looking southwards towards Central Pier in 1890,
most of the gardens have not yet been developed.
The photograph shows the early electric lighting and
the original single-track arrangement of the tramway,
before it was altered at the beginning of the 20th century.
[From Blackpool's Progress *1926]*

polygonal bay windows. In more minor streets the better houses might be two-storeyed with one- or two-storeyed bay windows; large areas of such housing would later fill the streets immediately to the east of the Claremont Park Estate (Fig 26). However, in a number of central streets the houses were smaller and opened directly on to the street and therefore had no bay window. Surviving late-19th-century examples can be found in Clyde Street, Francis Street and in streets flanking the railway lines running into Blackpool North (Fig 27). However, not all parts of central Blackpool had housing of this modest quality. By the mid-19th century Bonny's Estate between Central Station and Bonny Street was crammed with small, two-storeyed houses with narrow streets and alleys between them, in marked contrast to the large seafront houses on the other side of Bonny Street. This area was cleared at the beginning of the 1960s.

Figure 26
High Street, which runs northwards from Blackpool's earliest railway station, consists of two-storeyed houses with bay windows and some larger corner blocks.
[DP154918]

Figure 27
Enfield Road, which was built on the north side
of the railway line into Blackpool North Station,
probably in the 1880s, shows the simpler types of
houses that were being built for some of Blackpool's
rapidly growing residential population.
[DP154914]

The vast majority of Blackpool's houses employed a vocabulary of standard Victorian detailing, but from the late 1860s there was a short-lived adoption of Gothic detailing and gabled forms (Figs 28 and 29). On Pleasant Street, The Cliffs, a small Gothic villa, appears on the map of 1870, when it originally stood on its own. The same map shows the first villa of a small development using Gothic detailing in Chapel Street beside the railway into Central Station. A pair of semi-detached houses at 22–24 Park Road (Greenmount Villas) are dated 1878 and combined Gothic doorcases with the use of a shared central gable. Even Blackpool's humbler houses exhibited some familiarity with Gothic architecture. Regent Road has standard two-storeyed houses with single-storeyed bay windows, but the use of Gothic, pointed-arched doors distinguished them from similar nearby streets. In South Shore some of Dean Street's larger houses have Gothic doorways in otherwise standard Victorian houses.

Figure 28
At South Shore the original Parsonage with its prominent gabled form existed by 1870. It has now been converted into a restaurant.
[DP154863]

Figure 29
Cedar Villas, at the southern end of Cedar Square, has large gables and elaborate bargeboards and dates from before 1879. Homer Terrace, to the left of the modern sculpture, dates from 1865.
[DP154786]

Blackpool's housing stock was expanding to provide accommodation for its residential population, but it was also growing to meet the increasing accommodation needs of visitors. Guidebooks, trade directories and census returns demonstrate that during the 1850s and 1860s many, if not most, houses in the main streets provided visitors with lodgings and by the mid-1880s over half of households took in visitors. They also reveal that this was not an activity restricted to the wealthiest or poorest parts of the town. Many of the better houses in the town centre and on the seafront offered lodgings, as did some of the humblest streets in Bonny's Estate, beside Central Station.

Although Blackpool's growth included some areas of working-class housing, the majority of its new buildings and its entertainment facilities were clearly aimed at a middle-class market, despite Thomas Clifton's decision to abandon his development near the station. Blackpool still offered the type of small-scale facilities that had suited the genteel Georgian market, providing residents and visitors with an assembly room, baths, circulating libraries, fancy goods shops, bazaars, booksellers and rooms with billiard tables. The provision of bowling greens by hotels seems to have been a particular characteristic of the town and this early phenomenon is reflected in modern Blackpool where, in addition to municipal facilities, the Waterloo is the home of Crown Green bowling, and a number of other pubs, clubs and institutes still have their own greens (*see* Fig 20). Mid-19th-century guidebooks also pointed their customers to walks in the countryside and trips by sea and coach to the Lakes. Blackpool's guests were still enjoying the quieter, more sedate forms of entertainment, or were encouraged to enjoy them by the writers and publishers of the resort's guidebooks.

Blackpool in the 1860s

In the 1860s Blackpool was still small compared to England's leading resorts; in 1861 it had a population of almost 4,000 and a decade later it had increased to 7,000. In 1861 more than 20 English resorts were larger; Brighton had almost 80,000 inhabitants while Scarborough's population was 18,000. Nevertheless, by the end of the 1860s Blackpool was providing its visitors with two piers and a substantial luxury hotel, architectural projects that signalled an intention to compete with its larger and longer-established rivals.

In the mid-19th century the provision of suitable rail links underpinned many substantial developments. Since 1846 Blackpool had had a single track arriving at Talbot Road, and this route was doubled in 1865, though Preston remained a bottleneck that seems to have restricted the number of passengers. The provision of a second route to Blackpool would be key to the town's late-19th-century expansion. Work began on the line in September 1861 and the new Central Station, comprising little more than a cabin, opened in April 1863 (Fig 30; *see* Fig 12). The creation of this route would eventually allow millions

Figure 30
By the mid-20th century Blackpool Central Station had expanded until it could handle tens of thousands of passengers on a busy day.
[AFL03/Aeropictorial/R20518]

of visitors to reach the resort each year, but its most immediate impact was to shape the development of the southern part of Blackpool, providing a major barrier between seafront development and more inland areas (*see* Fig 40). The eventual size of the rail lines and the presence of industrial facilities including the gasworks, the electricity station and the tram depot would also lead to the streets near the tracks being filled with some of the most modest housing and cheaper lodgings (Fig 31). The other impact would be to stimulate later the

Figure 31
The railway line into Central Station was also used for freight and to supply the gasworks and electric power station that were established beside it.
[RAF/58/B/28, frame 5045]

creation of an area of large lodging and boarding houses to the east of Central Drive.

Despite the expansion of railway provision in the 1860s, it was still the smaller, more select middle-class market that investors in new facilities were seeking to attract. Blackpool's development had been unremarkable, but the construction of its first pier, North Pier, seems to have been a key step in a shift in its identity. Reports of the opening on 21 May 1863 appeared in more than 20 regional newspapers, including many beyond Blackpool's geographical hinterland, and trade directories of the 1860s featured lengthy descriptions of the new pier in their otherwise brief introductions to the town. The reason for the interest is that in the 1860s a pier was still a novelty and a significant technological achievement.

In the 1820s the chain piers at Leith and Brighton employed technology developed for the construction of suspension bridges, but it was the use of screw pile technology that ushered in the main phase of Victorian pier development. Eugenius Birch (1818–84) was the first engineer to recognise that this technology could be applied to the construction of seaside piers, and from 1853 to 1855 he built Margate's new jetty in place of a previous timber structure. Southport followed Margate's example in 1860 and Worthing's pier opened in 1862. Blackpool's pier was Birch's second and in June 1862 its first pile was driven in by the contractor Richard Laidlaw and Sons of Glasgow (Fig 32). The pier was much plainer than the one that exists today. Most seaside piers are now encrusted with amusements, shops and rides, but an impression of the atmosphere of an uncluttered Victorian promenade pier can still be enjoyed at Clevedon and Saltburn, both of which opened in 1869.

To allow steamers to land passengers at low tide, an extension was added to Blackpool's pier in 1868, and during the 1870s the pierhead was enlarged to accommodate the 2,000-seat Indian Pavilion, which opened in 1877. When the deck of North Pier was doubled in width in 1897, oriental motifs were introduced into the new structures on the pier and the simple mesh-backed benches along the sides of the pier were replaced by the elaborate cast-iron seats that survive today. The choice of an oriental style was influenced by Brighton West Pier, in which motifs from the nearby Royal Pavilion had been introduced, and thereafter a pier designer's vocabulary normally included exotic forms.

Figure 32
Originally the North Pier was a simple promenade pier with two pairs of square, wooden buildings with pyramid-shaped roofs at the landward end of the pier. On the rest of the pier there were three pairs of octagonal, wooden kiosks, with another at the pierhead.
[BB88/00110]

Blackpool's first pier was created for a select clientele, but the reality was very different; in 1863 it attracted 275,000 visitors, while in the following year 400,000 people walked along the pier (Fig 33). The success of the first pier attracted the attention of investors from outside Blackpool, and in deciding to open a second pier, Blackpool was rivalling Brighton, England's most developed resort. In 1864 the Blackpool South Jetty Company was formed to build the second pier, which was officially opened on 30 May 1868 (Fig 34). This new pier was aimed at a popular market, and the presence of a German band led to open-air dancing and helped to earn it the title of 'The People's Pier'. Its original form was inspired by its neighbour, with a series of small structures lining a simple promenade. These were relatively plain, although the finials on their roofs hint at a distant debt to Birch's more exuberant essay on Brighton's West Pier. The twin entrance buildings were replaced in 1877 by a

BLACKPOOL PIER.

Published by W. Porter. Fleetwood & Blackpool.

Banks & Cᵒ Edinᴿ

Figure 33
This engraving from an 1866 guidebook shows a
handful of well-dressed promenaders, the message
being that by paying 2d visitors would be guaranteed
a sedate, quiet stroll.
[From Porter's Guidebook to Blackpool *1866]*

central, main ticket office building, which employed an eclectic mix of vaguely medieval forms, and in 1903 the large 'White Pavilion' was constructed at the landward end of the pier.

The provision of a pair of piers suggests a growing ambition and confidence in what was still a relatively small town. In 1871 its population was less than a tenth of Brighton's, but this huge difference in scale would not prevent Blackpool from undertaking another project that might rival its south-coast counterpart. In 1863 the Blackpool Land, Building, and Hotel Company was established with a capital of £50,000, and it bought the 60-acre Claremont Park estate, a long, narrow strip of coastal land to the north of North Pier. Before the 1860s there was no road along the seafront or on the clifftops; the only structures in this area were some modest cottages where Cocker Street would later be created, and the Royal Edward Hotel, which had been built by 1845. This later became the Claremont Hotel and since the 1920s has been the Carlton Hotel. It was bought by the Blackpool Land Company, apparently with the intention of converting it into dwellings, though it seems to have remained in use as a hotel (Fig 35).

Figure 34
Central Pier, as it has been known since 1930, was designed by John Isaac Mawson and constructed by Laidlaw's, who had also built Blackpool's first pier. This Aerofilms photograph was taken in 1920 before the long jetty was removed.
[EPW002067]

Figure 35
The Carlton Hotel has an elaborate, wide façade with decorative gables, but old photographs show that the central, three-storeyed, two-bay part of the front with two-storeyed bay windows is part of the original, smaller, plainer hotel.
[DP154923]

Figure 36
Lansdowne Crescent's original design, using a tall centrepiece and end pavilions, echoes the grandest form of Georgian palace-fronted terraces. However, this has been partially disguised by later alterations to the roof line to provide additional accommodation. [DP154932]

The scheme for the Claremont Park Estate was to create houses and a hotel that would 'be the first resort of fashionable company'.[35] The exclusivity of this new development would be guaranteed by gates on the newly created seafront promenade at the north end of Carlton (or Carleton) Terrace and one at the north end of the development near the Gynn. Although the seafront road would be restricted to residents and people willing to pay the 1d toll, Warbreck Road (now Dickson Road), immediately to the east of the development, was open to the public and therefore this slender, exclusive development soon had lower-class neighbours in the streets being laid out to the east. To the south of the Carlton Hotel, Lansdowne Crescent was built from 1864 (Fig 36). This long crescent is the first example of a four-storeyed structure on the seafront, and its houses were adorned with three-storeyed bay windows. Construction of this height was limited in the 1860s to this crescent and the seafront's two largest hotels, the Imperial Hotel and the Clifton Hotel, but the economic growth of Blackpool would make four-storeyed houses more common in subsequent decades.

In 1863 a local newspaper article described the plans for future development. The intention was to erect a large building containing public baths and assembly room, with a hotel further north. Instead the Imperial Hotel was built where the baths and assembly room were to have been built, and they were dropped from the scheme as separate structures. The company had intended to build the major structures, but it expected to sell the rest of the land to developers who would erect terraces of houses, as well as detached and semi-detached houses.

The Imperial Hotel was built in 1866–7 by Clegg and Knowles, who were based in Manchester but had offices in Blackpool (Fig 37). Its original capacity

Figure 37
In 1904 a substantial extension was built on the north side of the Imperial Hotel by J D Broadbent, unbalancing the symmetry of the original design.
[DP154924]

was said to be 100 bedsteads in 120 rooms as well as restaurants, dining rooms, billiard rooms and coffee rooms. In 1881, when a company was formed to convert the hotel into a hydropathic hotel, it was said to have contained 130 bedrooms and 20 private sitting rooms. The increased size was the result of a new wing added by Mangnall and Littlewood in the mid-1870s. It provided 39 bedrooms and 6 sitting rooms, as well as a new restaurant and smoke room. The hotel was built in a French Renaissance style, and in its scale and style echoes grand hotels being built in Paris and London. Its only comparable contemporaries at seaside resorts in the 1860s were Brighton's Grand Hotel, which opened in 1864 with 260 bedrooms, and Scarborough's Grand Hotel, which opened in 1867 and was reputedly the largest hotel in Europe, with 300 bedrooms.

By 1870 Lansdowne Crescent, Adelaide Terrace, the Imperial Hotel and the first buildings on Wilton Parade and Derby Road to the north of the new Hotel had been built. The first small-scale developments along Warbreck Road behind Claremont Park were appearing, and in 1872 the Blackpool Sea Water Company was established to supply houses and businesses with seawater. The location of its pumping station behind the Imperial Hotel suggests that it was linked with the Claremont Estate, though it served the whole town. The newly refurbished and extended Metropole Hotel offered its guests hot and cold freshwater and seawater when it reopened in 1900, and the use of seawater in domestic accommodation was still a significant feature in the late 1930s when the bath in the flat in the Casino at the Pleasure Beach included a seawater tap.

Developments aimed at middle-class customers were also taking place in the centre of the resort. In 1864 the Lane Ends Hotel was demolished and a new building in an Italianate style opened in 1865 or 1866. The western part of the Clifton Arms Hotel was demolished in 1876 and had been rebuilt in an Italianate style by the following summer (Figs 38 and 39). Facilities for residents and visitors were also being added to the town. In July 1867 the Prince of Wales Arcade was opened on a site between the Beach and Royal hotels, and in the following year the Arcade and Assembly Room in Talbot Square were completed. It contained an arcade of shops, a restaurant, refreshment and billiard rooms and a saloon with a stage for theatrical performances.

Figure 38
For a few years the Clifton Arms Hotel had a rather lopsided appearance, the new, taller four-storeyed part dominating the smaller, three-storeyed Georgian block that was initially retained.
[From Blackpool's Progress *1926]*

Figure 39
In 1876 the Georgian block was demolished and the whole building provided with a more unified, external appearance.
[AA053251]

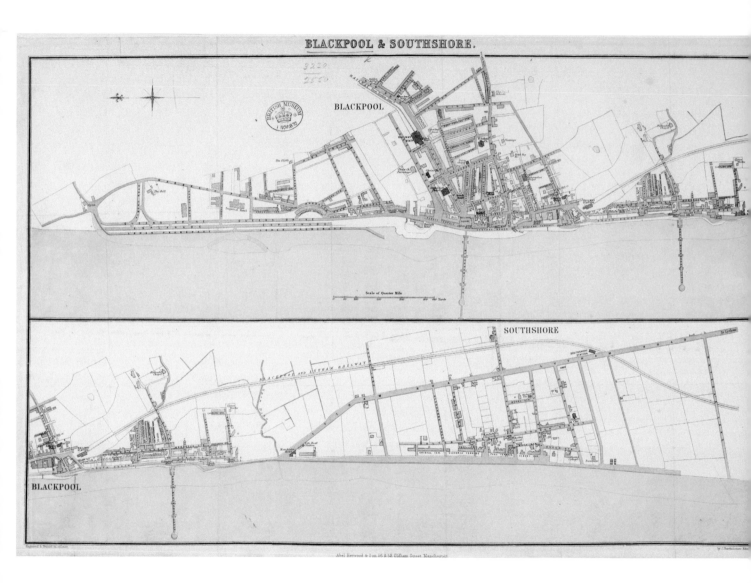

Figure 40
This map of 1870 shows the original settlement
of Blackpool in the upper strip, with the smaller
South Shore to the south in the lower part of the map.
The first elements of the development of North Shore are
also obvious, but, while some of the major streets may
have been laid out, few buildings had been erected yet.
[© The British Library Board Maps 3230 (4)]

Guidebooks in the mid-19th century reveal that a substantial proportion of the clergy and gentry in Blackpool chose to live in South Shore. Development there was not as rapid as in the central part of Blackpool; it was further from either of the railway stations, and it lacked the concentration of facilities that visitors could enjoy further north. The outline of its plan had been conditioned by the 18th-century enclosure and the road layout, meaning that by 1870 between Lytham Road and the sea there was a series of east-to-west roads creating blocks of development. With the construction of the railway in the early 1860s this arrangement was cut off from potential development further inland.

A 1870 map showed Blackpool as a small town, with most of its development concentrated between its two piers and stretching inland towards its first railway station (Fig 40). To the north the major features of the Claremont Park development were in place and at South Shore the key elements of the street layout had been established and piecemeal infilling had begun. The buildings of the town were predominantly two- and three-storeyed, with a handful of large hotels on the seafront to cater for its middle-class clientele. Blackpool's development had been unremarkable, but the provision of two piers and the construction of the Imperial Hotel before 1870 suggest that investors had confidence in Blackpool as a resort. In the following decades the newly formed corporation and private investors would combine to create a resort and attractions on an international scale.

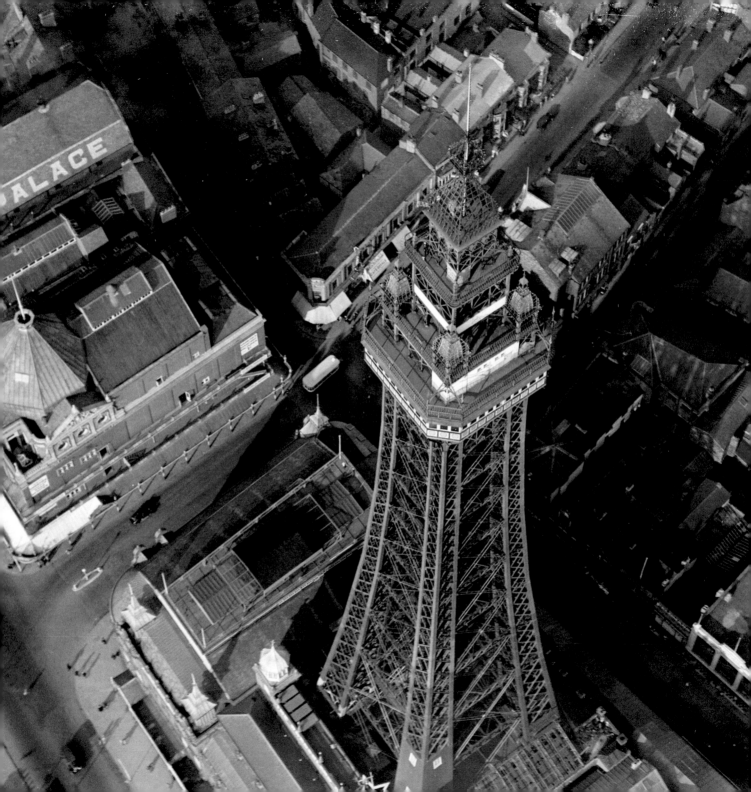

4

The rapid growth of Blackpool 1870–1914

Introduction

By 1876 Blackpool had grown sufficiently to become a municipal borough. The town's population was in the region of 10,000 and had been growing at around 30 to 50 per cent per decade, but in the years immediately before World War I its population grew much more rapidly, increasing by around 70 to 80 per cent per decade. In 1888 the Local Government Act allowed for the creation of county boroughs, meaning that larger settlements could become administratively independent from county councils. The threshold was set at 50,000 and once Blackpool passed this mark it became a county borough in 1904.

The rate of growth of Blackpool's resident population was outstripped by the rise in the number of visitors. In 1871 the Bank Holidays Act (34 Vict c.17) designated four additional days each year as holidays and these encouraged people to visit seaside resorts. Although this modest measure may have had an impact at some resorts, Blackpool already had a well-established pattern of holidaymaking, with the traditional Wakes Weeks meaning that the growing populace of entire industrial towns headed to the resort during specified weeks each year. Nevertheless, the 1870s saw the beginning of the rapid growth in the holiday habit, and Blackpool was one of the main beneficiaries of this new phenomenon (Fig 41).

By 1879 nearly a million people arrived annually by train, rising to almost 2 million in 1893 and nearly 4 million on the eve of World War I. The middle classes, who were the principal target for the major enterprises of the 1860s, now formed only a small part of Blackpool's visitors and the architecture of the town reflected this shift. The most direct expression of the growth in the holiday business was the reconstruction of the town's two major stations, North Station being rebuilt and enlarged in 1896–8 followed by Central Station in 1899–1901.

Blackpool's houses, churches and entertainment facilities also reflected the pace of its growth. Vast areas of late-Victorian housing graphically illustrate the increase of the town's population, while the lack of architectural consistency and the proliferation of small-scale developments reveal the absence of any central direction by a prominent landowner or a strong local authority. However, it is the creation before World War I of the Winter Gardens, the

This Aerofilms photograph, taken in 1929, provides an unusual view of Blackpool Tower and the adjacent Alhambra, which had become the Palace in 1904. [EPW029213]

Figure 41
This photograph by W & Co. Ltd was taken in c 1897
to make a postcard. It became legal to send picture
postcards through the post in 1894, the year the Tower
opened. The reconstruction of the promenade and
changes to the tram's power system at the end of the
19th century had not begun.
[OP00472]

Tower, the Pleasure Beach and a host of other ambitious entertainment venues that demonstrates the town's transformation from a modest, genteel resort to a place whose leading attraction could boast the title of 'The Wonderland of the World'.

Blackpool's entertainment facilities in the 1870s

The roots of the major entertainment complexes of the late 19th century can be traced back to developments in Blackpool in the 1860s and 1870s. During the 1860s Blackpool acquired its first two piers and Belle Vue Gardens was created on Whitegate Lane (now Whitegate Drive) as an inland destination for visitors. It was based loosely on Georgian pleasure gardens at seaside resorts and ultimately in London, though its immediate inspiration was probably its namesake, the Belle Vue Zoological Gardens in Manchester. Other small recreation grounds were also created, including the Castle Gardens at Carleton, the Oxford Pleasure Gardens at Great Marton and the Cherry Tree Gardens at Little Marton. In 1872 Raikes Hall Gardens opened for its first full season, providing its customers with fireworks, circus acts, dancing, acrobats and a range of other lively spectacles. An early edition of the newly established Blackpool *Gazette and News* in 1873 included an advertisement for Raikes Hall: 'These beautiful Gardens, 40 acres in extent, with their broad Walks, Drives, Fountains, Statuary, Terrace (600 feet in length), extensive Serpentine Walks, render them the most fashionable and agreeable place of resort in Blackpool.'[36] The gardens contained a large conservatory with exotic plants, ferns and flowers, a Grand Pavilion capable of accommodating 10,000 people and a dancing platform that could hold 4,000 people. Visitors could also enjoy a military band, evening firework displays and a tightrope walker, 'The Original African Blondin', who was 'The Son of the Desert'. The tone of the advertisement suggests it was aimed at a mass but respectable audience, but in 1874 the granting of a liquor licence led to complaints of drunkenness and prostitution, and the appearance later of fairground amusements suggest that the attraction was drifting downmarket (Fig 42). By 1901 the gardens had closed, the lake was being drained and streets of housing were replacing the park.

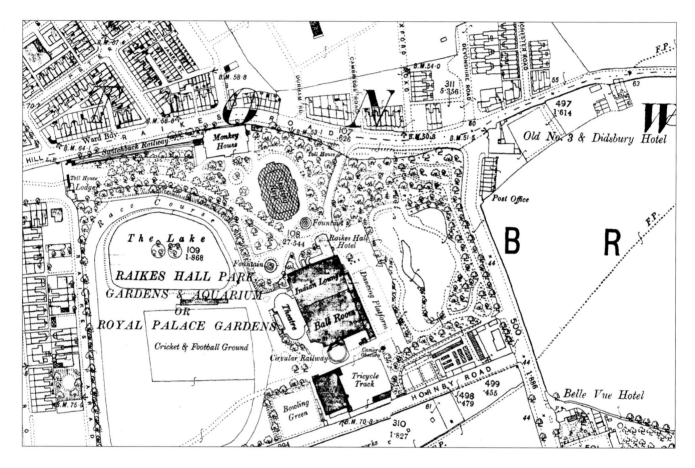

Raikes Hall demonstrates that the 1870s witnessed the beginnings of a significant change in the scale and character of the entertainments being provided. It also reveals that new technology had a role in shaping these facilities. Near the seafront, swimming baths opened on Cocker Street at the beginning of the 1870s and in the early 1880s the Prince of Wales Baths was created between the North and Central Piers, providing bathers and performers in aquatic shows with a large plunge pool beneath a glass roof supported on stone pillars. In 1875 an aquarium and menagerie was created on the seafront with three tanks in front for seals. Aquaria were still a novelty,

Figure 42
The 1893 Ordnance Survey map shows the substantial facilities available at the renamed Royal Palace Gardens. To the east can be seen the earlier, much smaller Belle Vue Gardens.

the world's first public marine aquarium having opened in Regent's Park in 1853. In 1872 Brighton became the first seaside resort to provide an aquarium, followed by Southport in 1874, Blackpool, Scarborough and Tynemouth in 1875 and Margate and Great Yarmouth in 1876.

The replacement of Blackpool's small-scale, genteel, sociable entertainment institutions with large, popular, reasonably affordable attractions was under way during the 1870s. In 1877 a large theatre was added to the end of the North Pier. This was a substantial venue, but when the Winter Gardens opened in 1878 they were on an even larger scale, creating Blackpool's first, almost industrial-scale entertainment facilities. The Blackpool Winter Gardens Company employed the Oldham architect Thomas Mitchell to build the Winter Gardens and by July 1878 it was open to the public, providing indoor attractions to enjoy during inclement weather. Blackpool's Winter Gardens belong to the first phase of winter garden developments that began in the 1870s and included large examples in the main north-west resorts, as well as at Bournemouth, Torquay and Tynemouth.

The Winter Gardens

The Winter Gardens is an unrivalled complex of entertainment venues, including some of the largest and grandest in Britain (Fig 43). The earliest surviving part is the foyer behind the Church Street façade, topped with its tall rotunda and dome. This leads through the Floral Hall to the horseshoe-shaped Grand Pavilion and Fernery, which had an iron-and-glass roof, providing a perfect environment for exotic plants and enjoying a sedate promenade. The Pavilion, which was at the heart of this original complex, was provided with a new proscenium and boxes in 1885 and was extensively altered in 1897 by Messrs Wylson and Long (Fig 44). In 1889 the first Opera House, capable of holding 2,500 people, was added. To compete with the newly opened Tower a series of new attractions was built in 1896. The huge Empress Ballroom was designed by Mangnall and Littlewood, while the adjacent Indian Lounge, an elegant refreshment room, 'eclipsing in splendour all the most gorgeously decorated Palaces of the East', was created by J M Bookbinder (Fig 45).[37] In 1965 it was transformed into a cabaret venue, the Planet Room. The Great

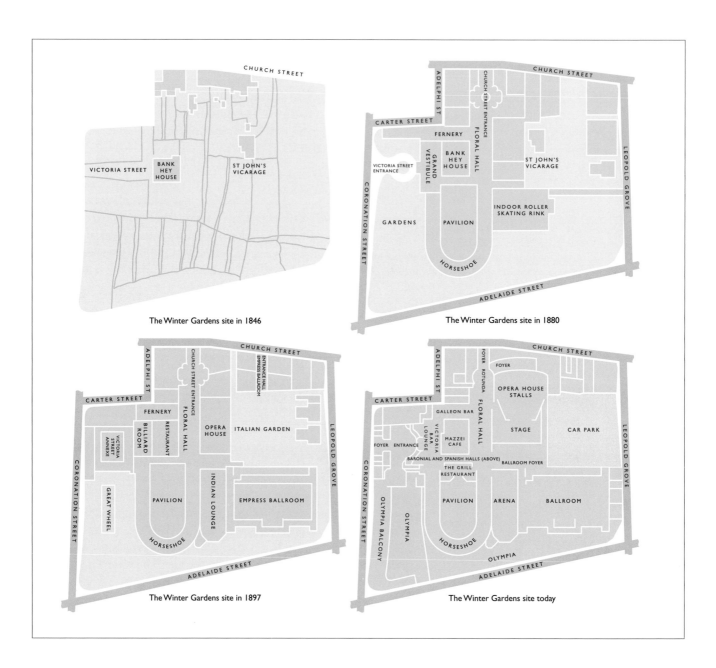

The Winter Gardens site in 1846

The Winter Gardens site in 1880

The Winter Gardens site in 1897

The Winter Gardens site today

Figure 43 (left)
These plans show how the Winter Gardens site has developed since the 1870s. Gardens remained prominent features until the 20th century, but today the whole site is filled with entertainment venues and ancillary facilities.

Figure 44 (right)
The alterations to the Pavilion in 1897 created an apsidal-ended music hall that could be opened out into the surrounding Horseshoe, explaining the claim in advertisements that it could hold over 10,000 people.
[From Blackpool's Progress *1926]*

Figure 45
The Empress Ballroom, which was built on the site of the original roller-skating rink, was designed to rival the original ballroom at the Tower, but was much larger and grander, prompting the refurbishment of the Tower's ballroom.
[DP117350]

Wheel, inspired by the Ferris Wheel first exhibited at the Chicago World's Fair in 1893, was created in 1896 on the site of the bowling green as a direct rival to the Tower (*see* Fig 53). In 1911 the second Opera House was built, and while it has been replaced, its magnificent foyer has survived on the first floor.

The takeover of the Blackpool Winter Gardens Company by the Tower Company in 1928 led to the removal of the wheel and the construction of the Olympia indoor amusement park and exhibition hall, which opened in 1930. Its façade and interior were clad in vast expanses of white faience, with blue and yellow decorative detailing made by Shaws of Darwen to the design of the Blackpool architect J C Derham. In 1931 a more extensive refurbishment of the Winter Gardens took place, with a series of themed rooms opening off the Floral Hall. The Spanish Hall was created by Andrew Mazzei, an art director in the British film industry (Fig 46). He also created the adjacent Baronial Hall, based on a Jacobean hall, and the Galleon Bar, with its plaster walls and ceiling designed to mimic oak timbers. Mazzei's interiors were deliberately whimsical, but Charles MacKeith's 3,000-seat Opera House, which opened in 1939, was a radical new departure (*see* Fig 89).

Visitors were taken on a journey – inspired by international exhibitions and current fashions – from India to Spain, from pirates to princes, from extravagant High Victorian to elegant Streamline Moderne. However, by the early 21st century the Winter Gardens complex was in need of restoration and repair. In 2010 Blackpool Council was able to purchase the site and has embarked on an ambitious programme to guarantee that the Winter Gardens will remain a key attraction for visitors and an important facility for the town's population. This initiative has already restored the Floral Hall of the Winter Gardens to its former glory.

Progress

When Blackpool became a municipal borough it adopted the word 'Progress' as its town motto. The Aquarium and Winter Gardens prove that Blackpool was beginning to be among the leaders in adopting new technologies and attractions, and its pioneering spirit can be seen in its early, if premature, use of electric lighting and trams. Official guidebooks demonstrate the town's pride

Figure 46
Mazzei's Spanish Hall has plasterwork around its ceiling that includes a frieze depicting an Andalusian village.
[DP117412]

in its innovative approach to electricity and this affection was reflected in the decision to incorporate a motif representing electricity in the town's coat of arms in 1899.

Arc lighting had been pioneered by Humphrey Davy in the early 19th century and had been first used in lighthouses in the late 1850s. This type of light was set up to prevent night attacks during the siege of Paris in 1870–1 and, inspired by their success, Paris became one of the first places to employ

Figure 47
This photograph, taken between the opening of the Tower in 1894 and the reorganisation of the trams and the promenade a few years later, shows holidaymakers strolling along the promenade, with the tall electric lights in the background.
[CC79/00487]

them for street lighting. In 1878 arc lights were installed in central Berlin and Jablochoff candles were used to light the Thames Embankment; the following year Siemens' improved lights went on display at the Berlin Trade Fair. In September 1879 nine Siemens lamps, each producing 6,000 candlepower, were mounted on lampposts that were 60ft (18.3m) high along Blackpool's central seafront, powered by an engine and dynamos behind Victoria Street (Fig 47). This was not Blackpool's first electric lighting: Raikes Hall and the Winter Gardens had installed lights earlier in the year. However, the adoption of even the improved form of arc lighting proved premature, as by 1880 the invention of incandescent lighting would eventually render arc lights redundant.

Blackpool was also forward-looking regarding the provision of an electric tramway. In the 1879 Berlin Trade Fair a small electric railway transported 90,000 visitors around a 300m-long track, and by 1881 the world's first practical service with overhead wires was in operation in the city. In 1883 Volks' Electric Railway, the oldest electrically driven service still in use, opened on the seafront in Brighton, and later in the year a service was inaugurated from Portrush to the Giant's Causeway in Northern Ireland. Most early electric-powered services relied on the transmission of power via their rails and wheels, but the Blackpool system, installed by September 1885 by the Halifax engineer Michael Holroyd Smith, drew its power from a conductor rail in a conduit between the rails. Initially the 2-mile (3km) -long service ran on a single track with a number of passing places (*see* Fig 25). This arrangement can be seen in a number of early photographs, but by the end of the 1880s the limitations of the power supply system had been recognised. Water caused the electrical supply to be earthed and sand collected in the conduit. Therefore, Blackpool followed other towns in employing collectors to draw power from overhead trolley wires. In 1897 an extension of the tram system to Lytham took place using Britain's first, short-lived, gas-powered trams, and a new line with overhead wires opened in 1898 between central Blackpool and Fleetwood. The switchover of power transmission systems in the original line, which took place between 1899 and 1905, was accompanied by the doubling of the tracks. Therefore, the promenade was widened and new sea defences were created, much as the renewal of the tram service in the early 21st century has coincided with new defences and an expanded promenade.

Figure 48
After World War I the former storage yard to the south
of the gasworks was also used for trams, and in 1935
this larger main depot was built on the site.
[AA053295]

Blackpool's early power station was on West Caroline Street (now Shannon Street) near the Corporation Gas Works. Located beside the railway line running into Central Station, this was convenient for delivering the coal required for power generation (*see* Fig 31). In October 1893 Lord Kelvin ceremonially switched on the machinery in the new electricity works. The Tower, which was structurally complete but not yet open, was to be illuminated by thousands of lights, though heavy rain meant that not all the circuitry worked. In 1885 the same area had been chosen as the location for the first, small tram depot, which was sandwiched between the gasworks and Blundell Street. It was substantially rebuilt in 1899, and this building survived until 1982 (Fig 48).

Blackpool's entertainment industry at the end of the 19th century

An advertisement in the Blackpool *Gazette and News* in July 1899 summarised the major attractions available to visitors. They could enjoy the Winter Gardens including the recently opened Empress Ballroom and Opera House, the Grand Theatre, the Empire (renamed the Hippodrome in 1900), the Alhambra, three piers and the Tower. Blackpool's leading attractions were creations of the previous decade or had been subject to major alterations during the 1890s, and vast areas of new housing and larger hotels had been added to the town during the 1880s and 1890s. One article in the local newspaper recorded how 'Improvement and extension seem to be running riot in Blackpool just now. On every hand are the workmen to be seen in every street and in every house, almost.'[38] Having acknowledged this new role for monumental entertainment facilities, it is interesting to note that official guidebooks at the beginning of the 20th century were still promoting Blackpool as a health resort. The 1906 guidebook *Blackpool: home of health, paradise of pleasure* emphasised the twin virtues of the town, until the Corporation's publicity department plumped for the more prosaic title *Official guide* on the eve of World War I.

The sudden growth in the size and number of Blackpool's entertainment facilities was initiated by the opening in June 1889 of the first Opera House, designed by Frank Matcham, at the Winter Gardens. He was already an

Figure 49
Thomas Sergenson was the 'spirited entrepreneur'
behind the Grand Theatre, which replaced the
Grand Circus with a new theatre capable of holding
3,000 customers in an elegant interior with ornate
crush-rooms, foyers and saloons.
[AA053253]

accomplished designer of theatres, his first solo commission having been completed in 1879, and was also responsible for the Grand Theatre, dubbed 'Matcham's masterpiece' when it opened in July 1894 (Fig 49).[39] On the seafront the third pier, Victoria Pier, opened in 1893 at the south end of the resort, where South Shore had been developing quickly (Fig 50). The exotic appearance of the new pier seems to have been the reason that in 1896 the once relatively plain North Pier was doubled in width and provided with elaborate kiosks with oriental-influenced roofs.

These new attractions were aimed at catering for the rapidly growing numbers of visitors to Blackpool, and the opening of the Tower in May 1894 was the ultimate expression of the scale that its holidaymaking infrastructure had reached. It exemplified the mass production of fun, providing customers with lavish interiors at an affordable price, relying on millions of visitors to make a profit. Blackpool Tower was also a technical triumph and an act of financial courage, particularly by John Bickerstaffe, mayor of Blackpool and chairman of the Tower Company. Designed by the Manchester-based practice of Maxwell and Tuke, the Tower, which was Britain's tallest building when it was built, measured 518ft 9in (158m) to the top of the flagstaff and was constructed in less than three years at a cost of £300,000 (Fig 51). Its first guidebook was naturally effusive about the whole venture:

> The successful erection of the Tower, in itself one of the greatest engineering feats of modern times, forms only one portion of their gigantic undertaking. To this must be added the completion of the extensive block of buildings clustered round the Tower basement, another great triumph of the architect's art and the builder's skill.[40]

The Tower represented a major threat to the Winter Gardens, whose management in 1896 reacted by improving its facilities. To attract customers the huge Empress Ballroom was built on the site of the original roller-skating rink, and at the other end of the site the Great Wheel was created on the site of the bowling green (Fig 52).

The Tower also faced competition from a new rival being created on the seafront. The Alhambra was designed by Wylson and Long of London and its foundation stone was laid in December 1897 (Fig 53). A commemorative

Victoria Pier. Blackpool. W. 4058.

Figure 50
*Victoria Pier – renamed South Pier in 1930 – was
encrusted with oriental-influenced kiosks as well as
a theatre at its seaward end, which was destroyed by
fire in 1958. Its replacement was demolished to make
way for fairground rides.*
[OP00487]

Figure 51
The 1895 guide to the recently opened Tower described it thus: 'The bright and cheerful impression conveyed by the whole, results from the extensive use of Ruabon brick and terra-cotta, materials which experience has shown to be admirably fitted to resist the action of sand and rain storms.'
[AA058315]

guidebook in 1899 stated that its theatre could hold an audience of 3,000, though the local newspaper claimed 5,000 with 3,500 being seated; the Circus had a capacity of 2,000 and the 'most enchanting Ballroom in all Europe' catered for 3,000 people or 500 couples dancing.[41] There was also a restaurant, lounges, roof promenades and balconies that catered for several thousand more customers. The same advertisement hailed it as: 'The newest of the new! Modern Comfort and Eastern Luxury', and its interiors were rightly famed for their lavishness. At the heart of the public spaces were marble halls, with floors laid with Italian marble and Venetian mosaic, while the stairs were built using solid Carrara marble. The Alhambra opened in August 1899, but went

Figure 52
The wheel was 220ft (67m) high, with an axle 41ft (12m) long, and had 30 carriages, each carrying around 30 people who had paid 6d for the experience. It lasted for over 30 years until it was dismantled in 1929.
[OP00489]

The Tower & Wheel, Blackpool.

JWS 2333

Figure 53
The Alhambra occupied the site to the north of the
Tower. The presence of its name on the roof suggests
the photograph may predate its reopening as the
Palace in 1904.
[BB88/00113]

bankrupt in November 1902. The building was acquired by the Blackpool Tower Company and reopened as the Palace in July 1904 following a redesign of its interiors by Frank Matcham. It was demolished in 1962 and replaced by a large department store.

Blackpool Tower

The foundation stone of Blackpool Tower was laid on 25 September 1891, and by early 1893 the structure of the Tower had begun to rise above the roofline of the building being constructed around its base. The Tower building opened to the public on 14 May 1894 (Fig 54).

Blackpool Tower offered visitors a range of entertainments for 6d. For this fee they could visit an aquarium decorated with columns of rough rock supporting a cavern-like ceiling, a menagerie holding big cats and other creatures, a monkey house and aviary, a seal pond and bear cage, and roof gardens. The Tower's elevator hall was treated as a picturesque English village; there was also a grand saloon, a refreshment bar, a billiard saloon and the Grand Pavilion, which would soon be reinvented as the celebrated Tower Ballroom. If visitors paid extra they could ascend the Tower or enjoy a show in the 3,000-seat Circus (Fig 55). The floor of the Circus could be lowered to reveal a 6ft 6in-deep water tank for aquatic performances. This type of arrangement had been pioneered in 1871 at the Cirque in Argyll Street in London, which closed in 1909.

In response to the enlarged Winter Gardens, the lavish Alhambra and the Hippodrome, Frank Matcham was employed to transform the Tower's main venues between 1898 and 1904. By 1899 the ballroom had been extended and raised in height by Maxwell and Tuke (Fig 56). Matcham employed a white-and-gold paint scheme in the Tower Café, which incorporated gold leaf on some surfaces. In 1900 the layout of the Circus was altered and in 1904 Matcham completed the transformation of Ye Olde English Village into Chinatown. Although most of this work has been replaced, fragments of this complex decorative scheme have survived in what was originally the Oriental Arcade and later became an exhibition space dedicated to Charlie Cairoli's career.

Figure 54
By September 1893 the main structure of the Tower was complete. It contained 2,493 tons of steel and 93 tons of cast iron, while the structure of the Tower Building required a further 987 tons of steel and 259 tons of cast iron.
[DP034510]

Figure 55 (above left)
Frank Matcham transformed the interior of the
Tower Circus in 1900 into a Moorish fantasy, covering
up the tower's legs, which used to be more obvious,
in each corner.
[AA048176]

Figure 56 (above right)
In 1899 the stage in the Tower Ballroom was moved
from the side to the end of the room and a sliding ceiling
was provided to ventilate the room. Frank Matcham
adorned the new structure with lavish rococo detailing,
creating a sumptuous interior that was faithfully
restored after the 1956 fire.
[AA048180]

In December 1956 the ballroom was badly damaged by fire and the Tower Company decided to reinstate the ballroom. To restore the plasterwork and repaint the ceiling murals, craftsmen were brought out of retirement, including Andrew Mazzei, who had created the atmospheric interiors at the Winter Gardens. The ballroom reopened in May 1958. It remains a popular venue for dancing and its celebrated Wurlitzer organ still rises dramatically from below the stage. By the 1960s the menagerie was considered unsuitable for large animals and became a cabaret bar in 1963. It now forms part of the Tower Dungeon.

In 2010 Blackpool Council purchased the Tower and has begun a major investment programme. The operator Merlin has taken over the running of the complex and has breathed new life into it; to attract new visitors it has introduced a Dungeon and a 4D cinema.

Catering for visitors in the late 19th century

The immodestly titled guidebook *Blackpool: the unrivalled seaside resort for health and leisure* claimed in 1897 that the resort had 10,000 places for visitors to stay, presumably rooms rather than premises, at a time when the town's population was around 45,000 and the larger Parliamentary Division only contained 22,000 buildings (Fig 57).[42] The guidebook classified accommodation into three categories:

1 Hotels, Hydros and Boarding Houses, offering inclusive rates for meals and room
2 Private Apartments, where the rate quoted was for a room, with meals cooked by a landlord or landlady using ingredients provided by the guests
3 Company Houses, lodging houses where guests rented a room or bed and could either buy their own food to be cooked and served in their rooms or in a dining room, or dine out.

Figure 57
In the streets to the east of Central Station, which would be to the right of this photograph, hundreds of houses were built in the late 19th century for use as lodgings and boarding houses.
[DP154967]

Figure 58
The rebuilt and enlarged Queens Hotel is asymmetrical
in layout and is built in a vaguely Jacobean style,
its red brick enlivened with stone detailing,
including three-storeyed bay windows.
[DP154861]

The hotels and hydros were predominantly purpose-built structures, though some hotels may have been set up in houses or amalgamations of houses, an arrangement still employed in many of Blackpool's hotels today. The grandest hotel was still the Imperial Hotel, while the construction of the western part of the Clifton Arms Hotel during the 1870s created the building that exists today. On the seafront beside Central Station the Palatine Hotel was built in the late 1870s, providing 100 rooms in a large, Franco-Italian style block decorated with polychrome brick. Further south the South Shore Hydropathic Establishment was established in 1882, apparently inspired by the success of the Imperial Hotel's conversion to hydropathy. It was rebuilt in 1897–8 as the Queen's Hydro Hotel (Fig 58).

However, at the end of the 19th century most hotels were smaller in size or were modernised older buildings (Fig 59). In 1900 the Metropole Hotel reopened after a year-long refurbishment. This provided its guests with lavish facilities including a Moorish-style lounge, a Louis XV-style drawing room and a main dining room in a Georgian style (Fig 60). The ground floor also contained a ballroom, a restaurant and smoking and billiard rooms. As well as bedrooms on the upper floors, there were suites of apartments with a sitting room and one or more bedrooms and a bathroom.

Figure 59
The Metropole Hotel began life in the late 18th century
as Bailey's Hotel and was refurbished and extended
northwards during the 19th century.
[From Blackpool's Progress *1926]*

The boarding houses, private apartments and company houses provided visitors with accommodation in buildings that were essentially domestic in plan and appearance. However, during the late 19th century these increased in size, so that some three- or four-storeyed 'houses' on large plots were providing substantial amounts of accommodation. As early as the 1860s Lansdowne Crescent had been built as a three- and four-storeyed crescent and by 1871 most of its houses were in use as lodging houses or boarding houses (*see* Fig 36). By the 1870s large three- or four-storeyed buildings were also appearing in the centre of Blackpool (Fig 61). On Adelaide Street, which had been laid out by 1878, a number of three-storeyed houses with basements were erected, probably around 1880, and included bay windows with decorative

Figure 60
The lavish interior of the dining room of the
Metropole Hotel was photographed by Bedford Lemere
in November 1900, shortly after the hotel reopened.
[BL16201]

Figure 61
At the corner of Dickson Road and Queen Street there
is a short terrace of large, three-storeyed houses with
original attics, which appears on an 1878 map.
As befits houses of that date, there is a nod to
Gothic architecture in the detailing of the doorcases.
When built, the houses would have been beside
Blackpool's original railway station.
[DP154822]

shafts, a motif that had been employed on three-storeyed terraces at Imperial Terrace during the 1860s and on Eaves Terrace, which is dated 1878. A number of large, four-storeyed buildings with an enlarged footprint began to appear around 1880 (Fig 62). The central four houses of Tyldesley Terrace, which dates from 1880, are four-storeyed with three-storeyed bay windows, while to the north of this terrace old photographs show two terraces of four-storeyed houses that have now been demolished. At North Shore, the terrace immediately to the north of the Imperial Hotel dates from between 1878 and 1893 and consists of large, four-storeyed houses with three-storeyed bay windows, the bottom two storeys of which have been transformed by the addition of long sun lounges.

Tall, large houses were not limited to the seafront; the district that evolved to the east of Central Station contains some of the largest lodging and boarding houses. The western end of Albert Road, which was laid out by 1878 and built during the following 20 years, has a riotous collection of houses that were used

Figure 62
St Chad's Terrace in South Shore, which has the date of 1891 in its central gable, is an example of four-storeyed houses with three-storeyed bay windows. [AA053250]

Figure 63
The houses in the central part of Albert Road, which
are now mostly bed and breakfasts and hotels, range
from three-storeyed structures with tall basements
and a range of later attics to some four-storeyed
houses with original attics and basements.
[DP154828]

as lodgings (Fig 63). As well as being tall, the houses are large in area and while domestic in form and plan their scale indicates that they were always expected to be used for visitor accommodation. More modest-sized, three-storeyed houses with two-storeyed bay windows were the basis for accommodation in other streets to the south of Albert Road and on the other side of the railway line into Central Station, behind the seafront at Central Pier (Fig 64).

The piecemeal nature of Blackpool's Victorian housing demonstrates the absence of any large landowner or strong local authority seeking to enforce uniformity beyond a minimal adherence to building regulations. However, the streets would have originally seemed more uniform – or, more accurately, less varied – as during the ensuing century individual proprietors have raised the buildings in various ways, added sun lounges and illuminated signs and decorated the exterior in various colours and with a range of finishes. Less

Figure 64 (left)
The proprietors of businesses on Charnley Road have used colour and signage to attract visitors. Although the bay windows look similar, the height of the buildings and the materials employed varied along the street.
[DP154792]

Figure 65 (below)
These houses beside the Gynn are among the earliest domestic buildings employing faience on a large scale. Between the wars it became a signature material for major hotels and housing schemes in the rapidly expanding areas to the north and south of the resort, and it adorns the west façade of the Winter Gardens.
[AA053283]

variety would have existed originally, because all the houses had to use the limited palette of affordable materials available for mass-produced Victorian domestic architecture. The treatment of doors might vary, the detail of bay windows might be different and for a short time at the end of the 19th century some houses were built in stone rather than brick. These houses employed the same vocabulary as housing that visitors would have seen in their home towns, but in Blackpool the buildings were more ornate without incurring too much expense, as well as larger in area and taller to maximise the number of visitors that could be absorbed. On the eve of World War I, faience began to be used to embellish otherwise standard Victorian architectural features. A terrace of houses facing the Gynn, built by 1912, has bay windows encrusted in faience, decorative pediments and ceramic panels, while its front doors shelter beneath porches with fluted columns (Fig 65).

The huge numbers of visitors created an equal demand for catering facilities, and old photographs show that individual restaurants were plentiful. There were also large restaurants and dining rooms in major hotels and entertainment complexes. In 1897 the Winter Gardens could offer the Grill

Room for chops and steaks and the Grand Buffet for lunches and dinners, while the Alhambra's restaurant and lounges could house 4,000 people at a time. There were also other commercial places to eat on a comparable scale. The British Workman Company, a temperance organisation established in 1878, offered teetotal visitors the Station Temperance Hotel opposite Central Station and the British Workman on South Beach. The two restaurants provided seating for 1,000 diners at a time and in 1889 dinners cost between 8d and 1s 6d, meaning that 'Visitors lodging in private houses will find it more convenient and economical to dine here than to provide for themselves.'[43]

Around 1900 a number of impressive new pubs were being built in rapidly growing neighbourhoods and some were also catering for visitors. The Sun Inn behind the seafront in South Shore, built in 1900, is a fairly standard-sized pub for a growing area of the town, but its location would have also attracted many visitors. The Empress Hotel is much larger. Located 300m inland behind Claremont Crescent, its location suggests that its size was a reflection of the growth of its neighbourhood, though some holidaymakers would have made their way to the hotel (Fig 66). The largest pub of the period was the Waterloo,

Figure 66
The Empress Hotel was built at the end of the 19th century in an extravagant neo-Jacobean style. Located on a street running northwards from the Talbot Road Railway Station, it would have attracted some visitors seeking cheaper accommodation than was available on the seafront.
[DP154912]

providing facilities for seaside visitors, though its main attraction was, and still is, the Crown Green bowling green behind, equipped with grandstands for spectators attending major championships (Fig 67).

In the late 19th and early 20th centuries a number of Blackpool's existing churches were enlarged or rebuilt and other places of worship were created to cope with the growing number of worshippers, including in 1896 an early example of a Spiritualist church in Albert Road capable of seating around 200 people. A larger and more architecturally coherent St John's Church was built in 1878 by Garlick, Park and Sykes in an Early English style (Fig 68). Holy Trinity Church at South Shore was rebuilt at the end of the 19th century by R Knill Freeman. In 1894 the eastern end of the Roman Catholic church was replaced by a lofty, spacious sanctuary and, to cater for Roman Catholic worshippers in South Shore, a new church was built on Lytham Road in 1890 (Fig 69). The expansion of existing churches and the provision of new places of worship, as much as the growing size of hotels and entertainment venues, serve as a clear indicator of the rapid late 19th-century growth of Blackpool.

Figure 67
The Waterloo, which opened in 1901, is an extravagant Edwardian essay combining Jacobean transomed windows, Tudor timber-framed gables and semicircular Georgian-style bay windows. The stall in front is bedecked with Blackpool FC flags.
[DP154956]

Figure 68
St John's Church today forms one side of a large
public square. Its graveyard has largely disappeared
and the church has been subdivided to create a
smaller place of worship.
[DP154784]

Figure 69
The Roman Catholic church, photographed from
the Tower, has its original nave and transepts of the
1850s and the later east end, the form of which was
inspired by the early-14th-century Octagon of
Ely Cathedral.
[DP154988]

Blackpool before World War I: looking to the future

Blackpool Pleasure Beach evolved from 1896 on a stretch of the shoreline occupied by a gypsy encampment (Fig 70). William Bean and his partner John Outhwaite, who had connections with the amusement business, purchased 30 acres of undeveloped land that would become the Pleasure Beach. A number of American rides were constructed including in 1896 the Hotchkiss Bicycle Railroad Ride, a hand-powered bicycle ride on a track. Sir Hiram Maxim's Captive Flying Machine, a large, rotating swing ride, was erected in 1904 and was a by-product of his efforts to achieve man-powered flight. A local newspaper article in July 1904 excitedly described the ride as 'Our New Toy' and recorded that the machine was capable of flying ten cigar-shaped carloads of passengers at almost 40mph during their two-minute trip.[44] The ride was

Figure 70
This view of the sand dunes dates from around 1905, by which time Sir Hiram Maxim's Captive Flying Machine and the River Caves had been built. It also shows the 1903 Switchback and the theatre at the end of the Victoria Pier in the distance.
[From Blackpool's Progress *1926]*

powered by two 50hp motors that rotated a central, 20-ton, tapering steel column (*see* Fig 74). The River Caves, an attraction of 1905 that came from Coney Island via Earl's Court, was a sedate ride on boats that floated around a series of exotic interiors; it survives today, though the interiors have been updated. In 1907 one of LaMarcus Adna Thompson's Scenic Railways was constructed and two years later William H Strickler's Velvet Coaster was built. In 1913 the first casino was erected in an oriental style that was reminiscent of continental casinos such as Monte Carlo, but it was covered in electric lights, a reflection of the extravagant lighting of Coney Island's parks. Although called the Casino, it was not a venue for gambling, but contained a restaurant, bar, shops, billiard tables and a theatre.

Cinema was one of the most obvious applications of electricity and new technology to entertainment. The first films seen in Blackpool were shown using Thomas Edison's Kinetoscope in November 1894, a year after it had been invented and a month after its first demonstration in London. This new contraption was a cabinet in which a short film was shown and only one viewer at a time could watch it. In early 1896 the first films were shown to an audience in London and on 29 June a film show took place in Blackpool at the Prince of Wales Theatre. At the Theatre Royal in Talbot Square a half-hour show of Lumière's Cinématographe was available to visitors during the summer of 1897. A number of the restored Mitchell and Kenyon films were shown at north-western seaside resorts, including Blackpool, to the people captured in the films, while an early film in the Pathé archive – predating the change to overhead power transmission and the doubling of the tracks, which began in 1899 – shows a tram on the promenade.

These early films were not meant to be shown in purpose-built facilities, but in any room that could be blacked out and hold a paying audience. The earliest purpose-built cinemas probably appeared between 1904 and 1906, but the Cinematograph Act 1909 (9 Edw. VII c.30) seems to have prompted an explosion in cinema construction. By the outbreak of World War I hundreds had been built and Blackpool had more than a dozen such venues, a mixture of purpose-built cinemas, cinemas within existing complexes such as the Alhambra, and theatres and other buildings showing films occasionally. The earliest surviving purpose-built cinema in Blackpool is the Royal Pavilion. It opened in 1909 on Rigby Road as a venue for A1 Animated Pictures, which

Figure 71
The Royal Pavilion, which could seat 1,000 customers,
seems to have had a rather plain, flat façade originally,
with the stepped profile behind presumably reflecting
the original layout of the auditorium.
[AA058157]

used to be in the nearby Colosseum (Fig 71). The Imperial Picture Palace on
Dickson Road opened in July 1913 and could hold 731 customers in its two-tier
auditorium. The Central Picture Theatre, a single-storeyed building with a
barrel-vaulted ceiling, opened in the same year on Central Drive (Fig 72).

Blackpool's innovative spirit also extended to embracing flying. In 1909
it was decided to hold the country's first aviation week, beginning on Monday
18 October, but Doncaster hastily arranged an event beginning on the
preceding Friday. Blackpool's programme was based on a series of challenges
with prizes, but, while it was competitive in format, it was celebratory in tone.
In 1910 a second aviation week was held at Blackpool, and after World War I
Blackpool continued to be a pioneer in aviation, including offering in 1919
Britain's first scheduled daily air service and developing one of the earliest
municipal aerodromes, at Stanley Park.

Figure 72
The Central Picture Theatre was the most architectural of the early surviving cinemas, though like all early cinema designs it was conceived externally with an elaborate façade with a functional box-like auditorium behind. Its name was emblazoned across its façade and its date is included at the apex of the gable.
[AA052999]

The Pleasure Beach

The Pleasure Beach is unique (Fig 73). Over the past century new attractions have been squeezed into the site, and as taller, faster rides were introduced they often straddled earlier, smaller amusements. Some foreign parks may now offer taller or faster rides, but there is no other park that still reflects so much of the history of fairground rides.

The title 'The Pleasure Beach' first appeared in advertisements in 1905, as the series of concessions that had accrued in the sand dunes during the previous decade began to be consolidated into a single, American-style amusement park. Sir Hiram Maxim's Captive Flying Machine (1904) and The River Caves (1905) have survived from this period, though they have been updated in the century since they were built.

Between the wars larger, faster and more complex roller coasters and rides were added. For instance, the Grand National is the only surviving twin-track roller coaster in Britain in which the two cars race against each other, past features named after fences on the Aintree racecourse. However, the most

Figure 73 (facing page)
This modern aerial photo shows clearly how the park's
designers have managed to retain many of the historic
structures while creating thrilling new rides. The Casino
is at the top of the photo, with Sir Hiram Maxim's
Captive Flying Machine nearby.
[NMR 17760/20]

Figure 74
This photograph of c 1950 illustrates how the early rides
were being accommodated among the new attractions
and the whole complex had been given a consistent
architectural identity during the 1930s.
[AFL03/Lilywhites/BLP45]

profound change to the Pleasure Beach began in 1933 when Leonard
Thompson, who had been running the park with his wife since the late 1920s,
decided to employ Joseph Emberton, a leading modernist architect (Fig 74).
He was charged with establishing a more unified appearance for the rides
and the buildings in the park, and this ambitious programme culminated
with the construction of the new Casino, which opened officially in May 1939
(*see* Fig 90).

After World War II the links between the Pleasure Beach and the USA
that had existed since the beginning of the 20th century continued, and a team
from Walt Disney visited Blackpool prior to the opening of Disneyland in
California. From the late 1950s a new wave of investment in the Pleasure
Beach began to yield significant new rides, including in 1958 the Wild Mouse,
the last major wooden roller coaster on the site, the Derby Racer in 1959 and
the Log Flume in 1967.

Figure 75
The Big One, a thrilling, mile-long ride, has a
235ft-high lift hill that propels the cars around
at over 70mph.
[DP022320]

During the late 20th century the types of rides offered in the park changed as new technologies to hold cars and riders on the tracks evolved, allowing faster, taller and more terrifying rides. This culminated in 1994 with the opening of the Big One, the world's tallest coaster at that date (Fig 75). Other new rides were also introduced, including the inverted roller coaster Infusion that came from Southport and takes suspended passengers over water and through water fountains.

Defending Blackpool

Between 1868 and 1870 an ambitious programme of embanked granite sea defences, stretching from Carlton Terrace in the north to South Shore in the south, was carried out (*see* Frontispiece and Fig 54). In 1876 sloping stone defences were created to prevent erosion to the cliffs on which the Claremont Park Estate was built, but in 1896 the local authority acquired the estate, removed the toll houses, extended the tramway northwards and replaced the ineffective earlier defences, a programme that was completed in 1899 at a cost of £145,000 (Fig 76).

The need to convert the power transmission system of the original seafront trams and the doubling of the tracks required the Blackpool Corporation to obtain an Act of Parliament in 1899 (62 & 63 Vict c.184) to widen the promenade and install new sea defences. By 1905 new defences stretching almost 2 miles (3km) from South Shore to Talbot Square had been built. The Princess Parade was completed in 1912 to link these new sea defences to those created to protect the Claremont Park Estate, and included elegant colonnades around the gardens of the Metropole Hotel. The provision of new coastal protection continued during the inter-war years to defend the coastline of the borough as its boundaries were extended northwards.

In 1905 the festivities to mark the completion of the central section of sea defences included motor speed trials along the new promenade. Again Blackpool was embracing and celebrating new technology, and, to mark the opening of the Princess Parade and the visit of Princess Louise in 1912, a programme of illuminations, including an illuminated tram, was staged.

Figure 76
This photograph, taken from the promontory around
Bailey's Hotel, shows the very modest, inadequate
sloping stone defences of 1876 and the southern toll
house of the estate in the distance on the road in
front of Carlton Terrace.
[CC78/00088]

A similar display was staged during the following year, but with the outbreak of war in 1914 the illuminations were suspended until 1925 after an outcry about such an overtly festive feature during serious times.

War broke out in 1914 at the climax of the holiday season. After an initial disruption to transport services they resumed, though at a reduced level. Although the holiday business would be sensitive to the war, other markets opened up for Blackpool's substantial holiday industry, including accommodating 2,000 Belgian refugees and 10,000 troops during the winter of 1914–15. Blackpool's location on the west coast meant that it was not under threat from enemy action, and despite wartime travel restrictions and increased rail fares, Blackpool was still able to cater for an active holiday market throughout the war.

5 Interwar Blackpool

Blackpool after 1918

The commercial future seemed to be glowing as Blackpool entered the 1920s, but the council was quick to realise that the resort would face new challenges. Growth could not be assumed to continue indefinitely without the novelty and progress that had marked the explosive expansion of the holiday trade in the pre-war decades. Voices in the council, especially councillors with vested interests in the holiday industry such as the long-serving Bickerstaffe brothers, insisted that the time was right to invest in Blackpool's infrastructure. The town's facilities needed to be modernised and expanded to make the resort more attractive to a wider range of visitors, and some order needed to be imposed on the results of the rapid, haphazard growth of the Victorian period. There would also be a key role for private businesses beyond simply updating their premises with new signage, erecting a few new buildings and giving a fresh coat of paint for ageing attractions. Major investment in key businesses such as the Winter Gardens and the Pleasure Beach would be needed to keep Blackpool at the forefront of British tourism.

The figure at the centre of the interwar push for expansion and innovation in the provision of town infrastructure was John Charles Robinson. Between 1920 and 1944, Robinson was Chief Architectural Assistant to the Borough Surveyors Francis Wood, Henry Banks and James Drake, and eventually became Borough Architect. He was part of a department, containing architectural and engineering staff, which managed the town's projects with proficiency and no small degree of design flair. Although drawings for many Corporation buildings were attributed to the respective surveyors under whom Robinson worked, they remained largely his work. His designs were rooted initially in a stylish but civically appropriate classicism, but from the mid-1930s an appreciation of more explicitly modernist ideas becomes evident.

The earliest priority for the Surveyor's Department after 1918 was the improvement and extension of the promenade and its sea defences, a continuation of the programme begun before World War I. A short stretch of sunken gardens running parallel to the promenade at the Gynn opened in 1915 and a stretch of 'Pulhamite' artificial rock cliffs 100ft (30m) high between the new gardens and the lower promenade followed in 1923. Between the Gynn and the Metropole Hotel, the steep drop between the road and tramway at

This Aerofilms photograph of 1929 shows the Open Air Baths, which had opened in 1923, with the Victoria Pier beyond.
[EPW029209]

the upper level and the lower promenade at sea level was remodelled during 1923–5 with a colonnaded 'middle walk', a covered promenade that utilised the pavement at the top of the three-tiered slope as its roof (Fig 77).

At the other end of the resort the construction of the South Promenade provided a significant extension of Blackpool's useable seafront and created a blank canvas for what was hoped to be high-status residential and hotel development. Before World War I, the area south of the Pleasure Beach remained largely in its natural state, but the extension of the promenade and the tramway southwards to the borough boundary was a logical decision for a booming resort that required extra seafront space to create new properties with valuable and coveted sea views. Work took place on the new roadway, tramway and sea defences between 1922 and 1926, and the scheme also included elaborate sunken gardens complete with rockeries and flowing streams, along with a large model yachting pond and stylish circular shelters. A bold layout for seafront streets was incorporated into the plan, with two crescents parallel to the sea on either side of the new Harrow Place, with Clifton Drive behind them, running from north to south between the railway line and the promenade. The masterplan was conceived in 1926 by the

Figure 77
The new arrangement that hardened the cliff surface to the north of North Pier consisted of Lower and Middle Walks as well as the promenade on which the tramway and road ran. This photograph shows the interwar Middle Walk with its Doric colonnades mixed with Pulhamite, a man-made rock effect. [DP154940]

Borough Surveyor Francis Wood and the landscape architect Thomas Mawson, who was retained as a consultant to the Corporation following his work at Stanley Park. It was designed to encourage the growth of an entirely new district, with hotel facilities on the seafront and private residential development behind. In 1927 Mawson described his vision of the town's Beaux-Arts extension:

> If the borough is to expand, as the council anticipate, to accommodate over a million people, drastic alterations will be necessary. At present the expansion of the town is more rapid than that of any other town in the kingdom ... it will be inferred that a thorough overhauling of the design of this great Lancashire holiday resort is demanded ... [the new southern extension] will assume the appearance of a garden city, and be protected from the strong winds by the hotel and terraces of the houses which continue for some distance along the promenade.[45]

By the early 1930s elements of this new 'garden city' had begun to take shape. The first tranche of hotel development along the northernmost crescent employed a classical style with decorative faience dressings, while some more idiosyncratic Moderne examples of private hotels and houses were erected along Clifton Drive (Fig 78). The opening of the Harrowside Sun Parlours in 1938 marked a later phase of municipal development on the promenade

Figure 78
This crescent of hotels along the southern promenade extension was constructed in the early 1930s as an adaptation of Thomas Mawson's original masterplan. [DP154870]

(Fig 79). This solarium and small-scale winter garden was a reflection of the fashionable interest in pursuing improved health through exposure to nature. Broadly traditional in its detailing, the building was laid out symmetrically as two long, rectangular pavilions on either side of a central block facing the model yachting pool that had been created as part of Mawson and Wood's scheme. In many ways this addition crystallised their vision perfectly, communicating the message that this area was for gentle pursuits and quiet repose for more affluent holidaymakers and residents. By the outbreak of World War II Mawson's scheme was far from complete and the community amenities that he had specified had not been built. Today most of the development along Clifton Drive consists of private detached housing dating from the 1960s to 1980s.

A key feature of this programme of southward expansion was the construction of the Open Air Baths, which opened in 1923 between the Victoria Pier and the Pleasure Beach (Fig 80). Blackpool Corporation embraced wholeheartedly the taste for outdoor swimming by providing probably the largest such facility in the world. The baths were designed to promote the outdoors, sport and good health, and their architecture was designed to convey this wholesome message. They were monumental in scale, catering on some days at the height of the season for over 20,000 visitors. The design consisted of a large pool, which was half built-up on its landward side with two colonnaded arms meeting at the main entrance where a large, central pavilion

Figure 79
The former Harrowside Sun Parlours, which opened in 1938, is now the Solaris Centre, a business and training centre focused on issues of renewable energy.
[AA053152]

Figure 80
The Blackpool Open Air Baths, like a swimming
amphitheatre, employed classical features to create
an atmosphere of grandeur as well as entertainment.
[AFL03/Lilywhites/BLP43]

building with a glazed dome proclaimed the grandeur of the project. This well-detailed classical building in the Beaux-Arts tradition employed rusticated masonry, pilasters and columns in a sombre Doric order and was as much a civic celebration as a leisure facility.

The creation of Stanley Park, the town's first substantial municipal park, was another scheme intended to broaden and improve the experience of Blackpool's visitors and residents. Opened in 1926, this was Thomas Mawson's first commission from the Corporation (Fig 81). He had already become well known for his landscape architecture work at Belle Vue Park in Newport (Wales) and at Lord Leverhulme's house, The Hill, in Hampstead. Creating a park located more than a mile from the seafront may seem an odd method of enhancing the experience of holidaymakers, but the rationale of the plan was spelled out by the Town Clerk, Trevor T Jones, as he looked back in 1939:

Blackpool dares not lose sight of the changing social habits of the people in its planning. At the time, the decision to lay out Stanley Park was probably most notable as an intention to provide outdoor facilities in face of opposition which held the catholic view that nothing should be done to take the visitor away from the Promenade and the shopping centre. I venture to say that Blackpool would have lost much of its popularity had the park not been provided when it was. Considering the advent in recent years of the working-class golfer and the artisan tennis player, what would have been their reaction to find that they could not enjoy their favourite games at their favourite holiday resort? Facilities must be provided ahead of the trend of social events.[46]

Jones might also have mentioned that the park was intended as a spur to high-class, private development around its perimeter, which would act as the centre of a middle-class residential district that would help to transform the image of the town.

Stanley Park differed from earlier large municipal parks as it was a park of activities with some open green spaces between them. Bowling greens, putting

Figure 81
The bandstand and boating lake are at the heart of Stanley Park, which combined formal planning and architecture with a multitude of areas for outdoor activity.
[DP157222]

greens, a cricket ground, playing fields, a boating lake, a bandstand, a golf course and tennis courts were all provided in a well-landscaped setting with a formal Italian water garden at its heart. A major civic centre and even a new town hall were considered as potential candidates for the centrepiece of the park, but budgetary constraints meant that plans for a focal building could not be realised immediately. Instead, a stylish café designed by J C Robinson, combining civic-minded classical proportions with more exuberant Moderne detailing, took the position at the head of the Italian gardens in 1937 (Fig 82).

The Corporation's investment in the town's infrastructure continued throughout the 1930s. The Cabin Lift of 1930 was a bold and visually striking solution to the problem of providing access to the sea and a new model-boating

Figure 82
The Stanley Park Café, designed by J C Robinson and opened in 1937, is the centrepiece of the park and combines a solid civic presence with playful art deco detailing internally.
[DP157226]

lake for visitors staying on the cliffs of the North Shore. J C Robinson's design for the lift tower employed classical detailing in faience applied to the stark brick structure, but it was the copper-clad, pyramidal roof topped with a flagpole that set the building up as a landmark. Half a mile to the south on the seafront the Derby Baths of 1939, named after local landowner the Earl of Derby, was a celebration of the civic pride of the Corporation. As with the earlier, outdoor baths, the design was inspired by classical forms, but the building was more austere and serious, with any hint of frivolity having been stripped right back to create a crisp modernity. Although the Derby Baths, the Cabin Lift and the boating pool were a long way from the attractions of the town centre, it was not only guests from the upmarket North Shore hotels who would have benefitted from the spread of resort features. The increase in visitor numbers by the 1930s and their growing mobility by car and improved public transport meant that other holidaymakers and day trippers could also enjoy these new facilities.

Changes in the means of transport used by visitors were recognised by the Corporation as potential problems that needed to be addressed. A gradual shift was already underway from travelling by train and staying for several nights to day-trippers arriving by car and coach, though the rate of change was to accelerate dramatically later in the 20th century. Creating enhanced provision for motor transport required a good degree of innovation in what was already a very built-up town, and in 1933 motorists were offered Britain's second underground car park (after Hastings) at Little Bispham. It provided a linear run of parking spaces integrated into the new promenade and sea defence work along the coast, accessed by in- and out-ramps. While this location was a long way to the north of the resort, the adjacent tramway meant that this served as a park-and-ride facility, a form of integrated transport system that anticipated late-20th-century schemes for relieving congestion.

Provision for motor vehicles was also being made in the town centre. Adjacent to the original site of Blackpool North Railway Station, the Surveyor's Department, with engineering by G W Stead, built a new bus station combined with the country's first municipal multi-storey car park. On its completion in 1939, the building provided parking on eight split levels over a double-height ground floor for the circulation of double-decker buses (Fig 83). Care was taken to imbue the structure with the dignity expected of a public building;

Figure 83
The original conception of the Talbot Road Bus Station and Car Park now seems commonplace, belying the innovation shown in the original structure of 1937–9. The exterior was re-clad in 1963.
[DP119488]

cream faience cladding was used with some green detailing, the colours of the livery of Blackpool Transport's bus and tram fleet. Regularly placed windows provided natural lighting, but they created the impression externally that this was a normal part of the streetscape, removing any sense of the utilitarian. The nearby Odeon cinema of 1939 was of similar scale and materials, and the two buildings formed an interesting modern development of the interwar town on either side of the railway station (Fig 84).

During the 1930s Blackpool's tram system was the subject of further investment and rationalisation at the same time as some other local authorities were beginning to close their networks. Two seafront tram stations from the 1930s at Bispham and Little Bispham, towards the north of the borough, serve as fragmentary evidence of a comprehensive but largely unrealised scheme

Figure 84
The Odeon was designed by Robert Bullivant of Harry Weedon and Partners. The structure consisted of a steel frame clad in brick, with coloured faience cladding.
[AA053269]

to modernise the municipal transport system under the design guidance of J C Robinson. Bispham, the larger of the two, was completed in 1932, while Little Bispham, further to the north, was completed in 1935. Both stations also served as shelters and public conveniences and Bispham had a ticket hall and indoor waiting rooms. Bispham was the more conservative in form, employing a typical early-1930s fusion of restrained classical features along with some Moderne elements (Fig 85). Three years later at Little Bispham the infiltration of modernism is obvious in this more balanced blend of the modern and classical (Fig 86). The station was bull-nosed at both ends in a classic device of Moderne practice, while the use of faience for its columns and other dressings recalls the best commercial versions of stylised, streamlined classicism from the period.

Figure 85 (facing page, top)
Bispham Tram Station, designed by J C Robinson, was completed in 1932. As part of the renewal of the tram service, which was completed in 2012, a raised platform was created to facilitate access to the new trams.
[DP157204]

Figure 86 (facing page, bottom)
Little Bispham Tram Station, completed in 1935, was another station designed by J C Robinson. As well as serving as a shelter it provided facilities behind for travellers and holidaymakers.
[DP157213]

Robinson's work was not limited to the improvement of facilities that would benefit tourists, but was also concerned with the enhancement of the facilities for residents. The significant increase in Blackpool's residential population between the wars demanded new municipal facilities, including schools and libraries, to meet the expectations of newcomers and to promote the town as a viable, modern place to live that was more than simply a series of seafront attractions. The architectural highlights of this policy were the two branch libraries at Bispham and Hawes Side, both opened in 1938 and were built with combined municipal health clinics, and therefore served as centres of public services to the north and south of the borough.

The creation of new facilities for visitors was not limited to the Corporation. Some of the major landmarks from the immediate post-war period were high-class hotels, especially in the North Shore area, which complemented the accommodation provided in guest houses near the railway stations and along the seafront in the centre of the town. The land to the north of the Gynn was laid out in a grid pattern behind the new Queen's Promenade after 1898, and its seafront was gradually filled with large private hotels similar in scale to the Imperial Hotel. The first to be constructed was the Savoy Hotel, which opened in 1915 (Fig 87). In the local press it was claimed to have an exceptionally high number of large windows conducive to the health of guests, and particular mention was made of its proximity to middle-class pursuits including golf courses, tennis courts and croquet lawns. A motor garage to the rear of the hotel in St George's Avenue was provided in 1915 for the servicing and parking of cars (*see* Fig 105). It was one of the earliest such facilities for hotel guests in the country and was a feature that would have appealed only to the richest section of society. The spread of large hotels along Queen's Promenade continued during the 1920s and 1930s. A short distance to the north of the Savoy, the Cliffs Hotel was begun in 1921 and extended considerably in the late 1930s (Fig 88). Further north, the monumental Norbreck Hydro was a creation largely of 1912, but Halstead Best, the leading local commercial architect of the period, added a huge northern block in 1933–4. In addition to these large seafront structures, other hotels were built in the form of terraces of tall, two-bay 'house' designs, as in Victorian developments along the central seafront. The difference in the interwar years was that the hotels were purpose-built and had no earlier history as houses.

Figure 87
The Savoy Hotel was designed by Tom G Lumb of Blackpool in an Edwardian Baroque style, and was finished in red Accrington brick and terracotta detailing. [AA053232]

One of the finest buildings to be built along Queen's Promenade was the Lancashire and Cheshire Miners' Welfare Convalescent Home, which opened in 1927 and provided its guests with the opportunity to recuperate and improve their health in a quiet setting. The architects, Bradshaw, Gass and Hope of Bolton, created a building that meshed English and French styles of the 18th century to create a 20th-century version of the pomp and symmetry of a grand hotel.

Development was not restricted to the newly colonised areas to the north and south of the resort, but was also taking place at Blackpool's best-known institutions. After the Winter Gardens was taken over by the Tower Company in 1928, an immediate programme of investment and expansion was overseen by the in-house architect, J C Derham, with Andrew Mazzei, who was an art director for major British film studios, acting as interior designer. Derham was responsible for the rapid creation of the Olympia exhibition halls on the site of the demolished Big Wheel. At the same time an elaborate new façade in white faience with rich classical detailing gave the newly expanded complex a visual unity along its Coronation Street and Adelaide Street frontages. Internally, a suite of bars and function rooms was created, mainly at first-floor level over the formerly double-height Coronation Street entrance. This allowed Mazzei's

Figure 88
The Cliffs Hotel was enlarged in the late 1930s by Halstead Best, who added a large tower with a shallow dome and doubled the accommodation provided in the hotel.
[AA053233]

genius for theatrical scene-setting to be given full expression in a sequence of historically themed rooms, which opened in 1931, with the Baronial and Spanish Halls as the entertaining culmination (*see* Fig 46). In 1939 the third Opera House within the complex was opened, with Charles MacKeith's designs bringing a modernistic tour de force to the Winter Gardens (Fig 89).

Innovative new architecture was also appearing at the Pleasure Beach. From 1933 Joseph Emberton undertook a programme to give the site a unified Moderne character by providing new structures and rides as well as cladding older ones with a veneer of modernity (*see* Fig 74). Foremost amongst the new buildings because of its position on the promenade, and the last to be

Figure 89
The third Opera House was the largest theatre in the country when it opened just before the outbreak of World War II. Its audience of 3,000 was surrounded by streamlined art deco forms and detailing.
[DP117386]

completed before war broke out, was the new Casino, which was designed by Emberton with assistance from Halstead Best (Fig 90). For a building dedicated to entertainment this was striking as an essay in uncompromising geometric discipline, with its glamour being derived from its sleekness and simplicity. The casino's circular plan steps upwards to provide levels of flat roofs for sunbathing, and inside is a series of open-plan spaces, fitted out with restaurants, dance floors and bars, as well as the administrative and other functions of the Pleasure Beach Company, including a flat for the Managing

Figure 90
The Casino building of the Pleasure Beach, completed in 1939, is the purest example in Blackpool of the International Style modernism that made tentative headway into English architecture during the 1930s.
[DP154856]

Director. A narrow spiral tower at the main entrance onto the Promenade serves as a strong vertical marker to what is a relatively squat building, acting almost like a flagpole and as a means to display vertical, illuminated lettering. It also served as a clear signal to visitors that this was a venue containing modern entertainments.

Away from the major entertainment complexes, some smaller-scale buildings were erected that reflected the adventurous architectural spirit of the period. These included the hotels, pubs, cafés, shops, apartments and cinemas that catered for residents and visitors. They also reflected the shifting tastes of architects, developers and the public and their desire for novelty. Some of the smaller buildings were more eye-catching than others, especially those located on the Promenade, such as the Lion Hotel, which opened in 1937 and was designed by Halstead Best (Fig 91). It resembled an art deco cinema in miniature, with a circular tower feature complete with streamlined fins at the centre of a strong symmetrical composition with bull-nosed ends and curved corners. Halstead Best also designed three pubs for the Thwaites Brewery that all opened in 1939. The Gynn Hotel, near the site of the historic Gynn Inn that had been demolished in 1921, was in a fairly traditional neo-Georgian style,

Figure 91
Although the Lion Hotel was only a two-storeyed building, it nevertheless employed modernist construction techniques, including a steel frame with flat, concrete roofs and floors. Its façade was originally finished in red brick with cream faience detailing.
[DP154860]

perhaps providing a faint homage to its lost Georgian predecessor, whereas the Fleece Hotel on Market Street and the Duke of York on Dickson Road employed pared-down versions of the modernity seen at the Lion Hotel. Particularly sad losses of pubs built in this period include two mini-masterpieces by J C Derham. The Little Vic on Victoria Street, built for Catterall and Swarbrick in 1933, allowed him to reprise his professional relationship with Andrew Mazzei. They created an imitation of a Spanish mountain tavern internally, with an art deco faience exterior topped with a central tower under a Spanish-style pyramidal roof with glazed pantiles. The 1936 replacement for the mid-19th-century Manchester Hotel eschewed any historical themes and was a triumphant example of up-to-date art deco showmanship. Situated on a key junction where the Promenade met Lytham Road, the pub acted as a major landmark and announced itself with a cluster of four prominent vertical fins topped with a flagpole.

Blackpool also had its share of new commercial buildings during the 1930s, including a number of smaller shops and commercial buildings in the town centre, such as on Topping Street and Deansgate, but it could also boast a rare example of a seafront department store. It was inevitable that the new Woolworths building of 1938, with its prominent position beside the Tower and occupying the site of the former Royal Hotel, would be on a scale seldom matched anywhere else and would be finished with a certain architectural flourish that would alert visitors and residents to the retail pleasures within (Fig 92 and *see* Fig 102). The new building, designed by Woolworths' in-house architect William Priddle, was nothing less than a shopping palace, with rich cream faience cladding and detailing in a stripped classical style, but with some more geometric Moderne touches. The Savoy Café, about 100m to the north on the promenade, was also located in a fresh new building for a new era, its façade being dominated by huge expanses of horizontal glazing. It was realised in 1938 by Derham, MacKeith and Partners, the practice that continued after Derham's death in 1936. The same firm built Lockhart's Café in 1937 in the centre of the principal shopping district. It was another multi-floor, daytime, eating venue with chic modern lines and a circular tower occupying its corner.

Prior to the outbreak of World War II, J C Robinson was able to sum up the progress that Blackpool had made since 1918:

Figure 92
Woolworths department store was built between
1936 and 1938 on a prominent site beside the Tower.
As well as retail floors, its two 2,000-seat cafés on the
upper floors were magnets for holidaymakers walking
along the promenade in search of affordable meals.
The Palace Disco of 1975 is in the foreground.
[AA053170]

> Blackpool has maintained its position as the premier seaside resort by
> looking ahead, and boldly adopting large schemes which have justified
> this optimism by attracting immense numbers of visitors, and an
> increasing number of residents. The early adoption of the Town Planning
> Act and the remodelling of the by-laws have had the effect of controlling
> the development of the town in an orderly manner, and ensuring a
> substantial type of building.

Robinson's excitement was not limited to the bald facts of growth, but included
enthusiasm for the means by which it had been achieved, through the adoption
of the latest architectural fashions. He concluded that this would continue to
give Blackpool the edge over its rivals:

> In a progressive County Borough it is natural that the acceptance of the
> modern style in architecture should have become almost general. There
> is still, however, a strong conservatism in clinging to the traditional styles
> in dwelling houses and inns, not only here but throughout the country.
> Although modern fabrics, furniture and bathrooms are in demand
> everywhere we are reluctant to part with the coal fire, the mock Tudor
> timber gables and even use imitation leaded light windows. Perhaps they
> are remaining symbols that an Englishman's home is his castle and in this
> machine age the castle of his dreams runs on four wheels. He is slowly
> acquiring the taste for those plain surfaces and straight lines which are
> customary in contemporary design and can be so elegant and pleasing, as
> seen at the Savoy Café, Odeon Cinema and other modern buildings which
> are transforming Blackpool into a very modern and sophisticated Queen
> of Seaside Resorts.[47]

It seems that the town's motto of 'Progress' could be harnessed to advance the
agenda of modernist ideas and should have pointed to an even more exciting
future, but the outbreak of World War II and fundamental changes to the
country, its people and holidaymaking after the war would make the late
20th century a challenging time for Britain's busiest resort.

Post-war

During World War II Blackpool's population increased as the town was still able
to function as a resort, but it also benefitted from an influx of civil servants and
military personnel who worked and lived in the town during the conflict. After
the war Blackpool remained a popular destination; the post-war economic
recovery and its continuing popularity meant that investment continued and
existing attractions were largely maintained and even enhanced. However,
from the 1960s, visitor numbers seem to have begun to decrease, and economic
decline, combined with grandiose planning visions that fell short of their
desired effect, has led to the loss of some historic buildings. To compound this,
the somewhat rare additions to Blackpool's resort structures were not always
of the highest quality.

After the war the Borough Surveyors Department of the Corporation had
begun to plan for a future that primarily involved the use of cars and coaches.
Blackpool's railway provision was severely curtailed in the 1960s, with Central
Station closing in 1964 and all major services being rerouted into Blackpool
North (*see* Figs 30 and 96). The site of the closed station was the subject of
various redevelopment plans until its eventual demolition in 1974, by which
time the long-mooted creation of a new civic centre on the site was already
underway. Edward Prentice Mawson, Thomas Mawson's son, had drawn up
a plan for the Corporation in 1933 in which the site would include a completely
rebuilt railway station and a civic square flanked with grand civic and
commercial buildings conceived as classical set pieces at the heart of a largely
rebuilt town centre. This plan was undone by World War II and changed
priorities, but a vision of a remodelled town centre was finally commissioned
from Tom Mellor and Partners in 1965. They produced a masterplan that
shared some of the popular themes being considered and introduced by
most major towns in Britain, including elevated pedestrian walkways above
the roads and new buildings stitched into a new system of circulation with
podiums and principle entrances at first-floor level. The realisation of the 1965
plan was limited and piecemeal. The police headquarters and courts complex
at the southern end of Bonny Street, which were opened in 1971 on land
previously occupied by infamous slum housing, were set on a podium above
a car park and connected to other proposed sections of the masterplan by

concrete and brick highwalks that could be extended when required. For holidaymakers to Blackpool, the principal impact of this redevelopment was in the area around the Palace Disco (now the Sands Resort) between Woolworths and Bank Hey Street (*see* Fig 92). Built in 1975 as the Palatine Buildings, it was provided with main entrances at first-floor level and was integrated into a system of highwalks that took pedestrians from the town centre over the seafront dual carriageway to the beach.

The rest of the land once occupied by the Central Station was used for car and coach parking, a direct exchange of public for private transport and the clearest indication that Blackpool would undergo a shift from week-long holidays by railway to more day-trip tourism. The landscape of the town was altered radically to accommodate this new pattern of visiting, but not by providing underground and multi-storey parking as J C Robinson had expected in the 1930s; instead, surface car parking became the norm where sites became available. The old Marton railway route from Preston was itself turned into major roads, Seasiders Way and Yeadon Way, the latter being elevated on the former railway viaducts. This route fed traffic into the heart of Blackpool from the end of the M55, which opened in 1975. The main railway terminus for the town was now Blackpool North. It was substantially altered in 1974 when the 1898 building was demolished, to be replaced with a modified version of the 1930s' excursion platform building further east. This structure with an exposed concrete frame, large gable-end windows and top lights can be seen as an updated version of a 19th-century iron railway shed.

In the post-war era some parts of the resort were renewed, though without the landmark pieces of architecture that had characterised the earlier evolution of Blackpool. Along the seafront, between Adelaide Street West beside the Tower and the Foxhall pub at the junction with Princess Street, there were substantial alterations to the historic fabric. After 1960 the rows of houses and commercial premises that had evolved piecemeal in the 19th century on the Golden Mile, with its famous stalls and sideshows, were replaced with large entertainment complexes. Venues such as amusement arcades, aquaria, waxworks and bingo halls were largely consolidated into substantial structures that were essentially industrial sheds in construction, offering large, unobstructed floor plans (Fig 93). To disguise the blandness of their form, they were provided with façades dressed with three-dimensional signage and light displays purveying themes from popular entertainment or evoking links to exotic foreign places.

Along the promenade, although few new landmarks were created after World War II, there were regular changes to the window dressing of entertainment venues, as the fascias, signage and lighting schemes reflected changing tastes and themes in popular culture. North Pier in particular went through a severe process of change with a chic, essentially new pavilion and signage in the 1960s being replaced by a full-blooded pastiche of the Victorian pier. The few major buildings that were built did make an impact and in their own way helped to shape the image of the modern resort. The rectangular sculptural features of the Palace Disco of 1975 added to the iconography of

Figure 93
The large, industrial-type units built along the central beach area after the 1960s swept away the narrow frontages and temporary stalls of this stretch of the promenade.
[DP154769]

the central Promenade by virtue of its proximity to Woolworths and the Tower, despite being a largely unremarkable concrete-framed box with dark brick infill (*see* Fig 92). The Sandcastle Waterpark was opened in 1986 on the site of the Open Air Baths, which had unfortunately been demolished in 1983 after it was decided that they were too expensive to maintain (Fig 94). The new swimming pool is one of Blackpool's key buildings of the later 20th century, both as a highly popular attraction on the promenade and as a landmark, with its sloping, cast-concrete walls, painted blue and arranged on a distinctive hexagonal plan.

Figure 94
The Sandcastle, which opened in June 1986, was one of the many modern, covered pools that were built during the 1980s to provide year-round swimming in place of older outdoor facilities.
[DP154864]

The challenges facing Blackpool in the late 20th century

> The Ministry of Housing and Local Government has issued no list for
> Blackpool, which means that there are no buildings of architectural or
> historic interest in the town. It depends, of course, on what one means by
> historical and by architectural. The historical interest should certainly not
> be denied. English social history of the second half of the 19th century and
> the first half of the 20th century cannot be written without Blackpool.[48]

In 1969 Nikolaus Pevsner was clear about Blackpool's historical significance,
even if the Ministry, limited by the legal definition of what constituted our
heritage, could not yet protect it. And Blackpool also enjoyed considerable
public affection; a 1972 visitor survey suggested that 6 million people made
16 million visits, but it also contained some worrying observations about
Blackpool's customers. Two-thirds of all visiting parties included someone
deemed to be old (ie older than 45), three-quarters came from lower social
groups (C2, D, E) and the majority came from Lancashire or neighbouring
counties. Nevertheless, the survey found that Blackpool still had a large and
prosperous tourism business, though some visitors were being deterred from
visiting by its perceived unfriendliness, dirtiness, lack of parks and gardens,
inadequate sports and recreation facilities and poor food.

In 1998 Professor John Walton published his book on Blackpool, a town
that he obviously loved, but he was acutely aware of the severe problems that
it faced. After World War II Blackpool had suffered from high rates of crime,
illegitimacy, seasonal unemployment, the poverty of old age, low wages and a
poor standard of housing. It also had an image problem, often being portrayed
as a town with benefits claimants filling its bed and breakfasts, polluted
beaches, drunkenness and litter.

In 1961 the town's population peaked at 153,185, but 30 years later it had
fallen to a post-war low of just under 140,000, though by 2001 it had risen
back to 142,283. There was also concern about the structure of the population.
In 2003 more than a quarter of the residents were over 60 years old, a figure
expected to increase in the future. The town's population also suffered serious
economic and social problems. Employment rates in Blackpool were worse
than the national average, and mean earnings in 2004 were only 72 per cent of

the English average and well below those for the region, a consequence of the town having fewer professional and managerial posts and more low-wage jobs. Blackpool's poverty was reflected in health statistics: in the central wards of the town almost a fifth of their population was recorded as not being in good health, compared to the national rate of 9 per cent. Crime was also higher in Blackpool. In 2004 the level of violent crime, car thefts and stealing from cars was almost 50 per cent higher than the Lancashire average.

Blackpool's housing stock faced serious problems. In 1992 there were more than 3,000 Houses in Multiple Occupation and in the following year over 4,000 (7.5 per cent) of private sector houses were unfit for human habitation and 24,500 (43.7 per cent) required substantial repairs. Almost a third of households did not have central heating, compared to the national average of 8.5 per cent. In 2001, the South Beach area, which included the historic settlement of South Shore, had almost a third of its population living in converted or shared houses, and a fifth occupied accommodation above shops.

Blackpool also had to recognise that its holiday industry was changing and visitor numbers appeared to be decreasing. None of the visitor statistics compiled for Blackpool, or any seaside resort, can be described as firm, but the trends in the figures are persuasive. In the 1930s an estimated 7 million people visited Blackpool each year and in 1972 6 million people made 16 million visits. A similar survey 15 years later found that around 7 million people made 12.4 million visits to Blackpool, with both day trips and overnight stays showing a significant decline. In 1999 there were around 13 million visits, after which the numbers fell to nearer 10 million, though in 2011 it was reported to have returned to the level it had enjoyed 12 years earlier. The holiday industry was still a business worth over £300 million in 1987, with almost 100,000 official bedspaces (Fig 95). In 1987 the occupancy rate for Blackpool's guest accommodation matched the national average, but with the reduction of visitor numbers it had declined to only 46 per cent by 2007. By 2008 Blackpool offered 60,000 bedspaces, 40 per cent fewer than in 1987, but further reductions of around a quarter in bedspaces and businesses would still be needed if Blackpool's accommodation was to match its visitor numbers. In addition there is the issue of whether the type of accommodation on offer meets the expectations of today's visitor.

Figure 95
York Street is still one of Blackpool's busiest streets of bed and breakfasts. Located behind Central Pier, it is near the industrial sites that were built in the late 19th century beside the railway into Central Station. [DP154847]

Accommodation requirements had decreased and changed, and there was an equally significant shift in how people travelled to Blackpool. For a century since the railways opened in 1846 the majority of visitors arrived by train, but after World War II the car became the dominant form of transport. The number of railway passengers arriving halved between 1962 and 1972, accelerated by, and reflected in, the closure of Blackpool Central Station in 1964 (Fig 96 and *see* Fig 30). A shift from bus and coach travel to the private car has led to the closure of the bus station on the ground floor of the 1939 Talbot Road Car Park (*see* Fig 83). The opening of the M55 in 1975 and Yeadon Way, connecting the M55 to the heart of Blackpool, in 1986 helped to cement the car as the

Figure 96
To accommodate the growing number of cars, the area once occupied by the Central Station became a car park. The former line of the railway leads to Blackpool FC's ground and ultimately links to the M55 via Yeadon Way. The station site was to have been the site of the casino.
[DP157231]

Figure 97
In September 2001 the monumental concrete walls
protecting the southern end of the Promenade at
the Pleasure Beach were officially opened. Unlike
the later defences, these were not designed to
allow easy access to the beach.
[DP154881]

main means of travel, and the cessation of a direct rail service to London in 2003 reflected Blackpool's increasing dependence on road transport.

Despite the problems facing Blackpool, significant public- and private-sector investment was still taking place. Major investments in the 1980s saw the creation of the Sandcastle swimming pool at a cost of £16 million, an indoor bowling rink and two ten-pin bowling complexes, as well as improvements to the Pembroke Hotel (now the Hilton), the Metropole Hotel, the Clifton Hotel and the Imperial Hotel. Money was also invested in the piers, the Winter Gardens between 1986 and 1989 and at the Tower in 1992, and the Sea Life Centre opened in August 1990. However, the largest private-sector investments were taking place at Blackpool's largest attraction, the Pleasure Beach. In 1990 £1 million was spent on the Grand National and a further £9 million was spent on creating the shops, restaurants, and attractions in the Ocean Boulevard, which faced on to the promenade. The largest new roller coaster was the Big One, which opened in 1994 at a cost of £12 million (*see* Fig 75).

At the end of the 20th century Blackpool faced considerable economic and social problems, but it also faced a major threat from the sea. Blackpool's geology means that it is vulnerable to coastal erosion; as early as 1788 William Hutton commented on this and by 1841 the first sea walls had been built to protect the coastline. Over the succeeding decades, and particularly at the beginning of the 20th century, sea walls were built, extended and rebuilt in a number of distinct campaigns. Nevertheless, these were still inadequate, and in 1981 a 20-year programme to strengthen the coastal defences began (Fig 97). The Shoreline Management Plan in 1999 indicated that there was also a need for new defences protecting the central area of Blackpool. Significant parts of the town's sea defences had less than five years of useful life and would cost tens of millions of pounds to replace. It was this monumental, urgent challenge that would galvanise Blackpool Council into action and lead to the launching of an ambitious programme of resort renewal that is still underway.

6

Blackpool in the early 21st century

This post-war image of Blackpool's crowded beach shows the Palatine Hotel beside the Woolworths building and the Palace to the north of the Tower prior to its replacement by Lewis' Department Store, which opened in 1964.
[AFL03/Lilywhites/BLP07]

Blackpool's Masterplan: A vision for the future

The threat from the sea recognised in 1999 prompted the development of Blackpool's Masterplan and the start of a £1 billion programme of regeneration. The Masterplan, which was published in March 2003, was described by English Heritage's Urban Panel as a 'bold attempt to ensure the future of the town'.[49] To breathe life into Blackpool's key resort institutions and areas, the Economic Development Zone (EDZ) was divided into four districts. For the Pleasure Beach district the Masterplan suggested creating a large aquarium in place of the Sandcastle Waterpark, beside a transformed South Pier. There would also be an 800-room casino resort hotel, an open-air park/event area, landscaped gardens, new parking and all-weather links to the rest of the town. In 'The Village', a cluster of Victorian hotels and guest houses, the Masterplan recognised the need for individual businesses to transform themselves by improving their facilities and exteriors, while the townscape, facilities and signage would be improved. The third district, dominated by the site of the former Central Station, might be suitable for the development of a casino or a water theme park inspired by the type of facilities available at a Center Parcs village, as well as large hotels. In the town centre it was hoped to get trams running along Talbot Road, and an improved transport hub would be developed with Blackpool North Station at its heart. The cleared area near the railway station would allow the creation of new office buildings, 300 townhouses, two new landscaped parks, three hotels and 700 parking spaces. The commercial and retail offer in the heart of Blackpool needed to improve to make the town attractive to people living in the Fylde, and new pedestrianised areas with restaurants and boutiques around a central plaza would complement a rejuvenated Hounds Hill shopping centre. Two other districts lying outside the EDZ were also identified and action plans were created for improving South Shore and North Shore.

The Masterplan contained other ideas that would inform Blackpool's subsequent development. It envisaged Blackpool as a 'resort of light': as well as its traditional autumnal illuminations it would have a year-round illumination scheme with state-of-the-art lighting and computer-animated light shows, inspired by Fremont Street in Las Vegas. There was also a desire to improve the open spaces within Blackpool and create a new, landscaped area in the central corridor alongside Seasiders Way to welcome visitors arriving by car from the M55 (Fig 98). A modern tram system would be created behind a new set of sea defences that would seek to improve the town's connection with the sea, rather than building a barrier between them. At the same time Blackpool's three piers would be improved and themed, with the North Pier offering a nostalgic experience, the Central Pier being the children's pier and the South Pier being the activity pier. This £1 billion plan was expected to last up to 15 years and to create 20,000 jobs.

Figure 98
Climbing walls welcome visitors arriving along Seasiders Way to the left, which occupies the route of the former railway line.
[DP154891]

Implementing the Masterplan

The first area tackled in the Masterplan was the Central Gateway alongside Seasiders Way and Yeadon Way, the route of the former railway line into Central Station. By 2006 arriving motorists were greeted by large areas of parking, climbing walls, a play area and new landscaping and planting. Subsequently this area has also benefitted from Blackpool FC's unfortunately brief spell in the Premier League, which provided funds to continue the reconstruction of its Bloomfield Road stadium.

In 2005 work began on the reconstruction of the central 3.2km of Blackpool's sea defences between North Pier and South Pier. Far from simply holding the line, as had been advocated in the Shoreline Management Plan, a bold scheme of advancement was undertaken. A series of five curved headlands reaching out into the sea, echoing the convex form of the coastline around the Metropole Hotel and the Sandcastle Waterpark, were created and the coastal defences were given a stepped profile to dissipate wave energy (Fig 99). Blackpool succeeded in making a virtue out of necessity by turning the five large headlands into areas for public entertainment, sports and performances. The northernmost headland, The Tower Festival Headland in front of Blackpool Tower, includes the 'Comedy Carpet', which opened in October 2011 (Fig 100). This celebration of Britain's rich comic past was designed by Gordon Young and contains the catchphrases, jokes and excerpts from famous sketches from over a thousand comedians of the past century. This headland is also used as a temporary outdoor arena capable of holding 20,000 spectators, and at its north end Festival House opened, housing the Tourist Information Office, a bistro and a small 'chapel' for celebrating weddings and civil partnerships (Fig 101). Another key feature of this stretch of the seafront is the creation of 'shared space', blending the domains of pedestrians with the tramway and the main road. This scheme is designed to encourage motorists to drive more slowly and give pedestrians greater ownership of the promenade. Gone is the intimidating dual carriageway that had to be crossed by a bridge near the Tower. Between the closure of Glasgow's tramway in 1962 and the opening of Manchester's new system three decades later, Blackpool alone continued to run a tram system, but this required modernisation. Therefore, a four-year programme was launched as part of

Figure 99
This design means that there was no need for a high sea wall; instead the stepped defences, combined with subtle shaping of grassed banks and lengths of contoured seating, were designed to prevent any overtopping from damaging seafront properties.
[DP157253]

Figure 100 (top right)
The Comedy Carpet took five years to complete. Each of the more than 160,000 letters had to be cut from granite or cobalt-blue concrete and cast into gleaming white concrete panels.
[DP154797]

Figure 101 (bottom right)
Festival House, designed by de Rijke Marsh Morgan, was one of the buildings included in the RIBA's Stirling Prize longlist in 2012.
[DP154810]

127

the promenade renewal to upgrade the track, provide new stations and build a new tram depot at Starr Gate at the southern end of the route (Fig 102).

The improvements to the promenade were completed in 2012, but some of the other projects outlined in the Masterplan have not advanced as quickly as first hoped. In November 2006 the Talbot Gateway Plan was approved. Its aim was to improve the experience for rail passengers arriving at Blackpool North Station, and sought to create a new transport interchange, as well as a new central business district containing offices, law courts, homes and a supermarket on derelict land to the south of the station. Along with an expansion of the Hounds Hill Shopping Centre this development would help to draw back retail expenditure into town. In November 2011 it was announced that Sainsbury's would open a 60,000 sq ft store with 600 car parking spaces, a key part of the council's £220 million plan to regenerate this part of the town.

In 2012 work began on this key part of Blackpool's vision for the future, but another area identified in the Masterplan has remained undeveloped. Since the closure of Blackpool Central Station in 1964, most of its site has been undeveloped. This site was earmarked as a possible location for a covered water park or potentially a casino (*see* Fig 96). By 2006 casinos had become the preferred driver for the regeneration of this area. In August 2006 Re: Blackpool, the regeneration company established by Blackpool Council and the North West Development Agency, submitted an outline planning application that included provision for two regional casinos and three hotels containing 769 rooms, as well as large areas of leisure and retail space and almost 3,000 car parking spaces. This was expected to cost between £200 million and £450 million, but would lead to between 4.2 million and 5.5 million extra visits per year and would create between 2,500 and 3,400 new jobs. However, the Gambling Act 2005 (2005 c.19) included provision for only one licence for a regional casino and when it was awarded in 2007 it was to be located in Manchester. The following year the concept of casino-led regeneration was abandoned completely. The loss of a casino as a driver has left Blackpool in search of private-sector investment to push forward the comprehensive redevelopment of the site.

Regeneration work was initially focused on the town centre and the promenade, but by the end of the first decade of the 21st century the council was beginning to address the problems facing North Beach, South Beach and

Figure 102
A fleet of computerised, articulated trams, each capable of holding 150 passengers, began running in April 2012, though some of the older 'heritage' trams still run as a tourist attraction.
[DP154779]

Foxhall. Supplementary Planning Documents are designed to recognise the problems facing each area, establish priorities for future development and direct appropriate intervention, following local consultation and based on a detailed understanding of the character of each area. Improving the public realm and introducing more green space and soft landscaping, combined with a recognition of the historic environment's role in the future of each area, are also key parts of each plan.

Although the major schemes arising from the Masterplan were aimed at providing new facilities and attractions for residents and visitors, Blackpool Council was also conscious of the important part that its rich heritage could play in its future. In 1969 Nikolaus Pevsner recorded with some bemusement the lack of any governmental recognition of Blackpool's heritage and in 1978 the Civic Trust wondered why Blackpool was one of only four local authorities that had not designated a conservation area, a power that it had enjoyed since the Civic Amenities Act (1967 c.69) in 1967. In 1984 two were established; one included Stanley Park and the large houses in the streets around it, while the other was focused on a small area around Talbot Square. In 2005 this conservation area was extended and renamed the Town Centre Conservation Area. To improve the fabric of its historic buildings a Townscape Heritage Initiative with £2.3 million to invest was launched in April 2006, initially for three years, though this was later extended until June 2012. At the same time as this was helping to improve the fabric of historic buildings, Blackpool Council was investing in the public realm through the pedestrianisation of the area between the Winter Gardens and St John's Church (*see* Fig 68). A café culture is developing in the town centre and new futuristic street lighting was introduced along Church Street and Corporation Street, while a disco-inspired lighting scheme and sound system has been introduced into Birley Street (Fig 103).

In 2006 Blackpool Council published its heritage strategy, which aimed to maintain, secure and celebrate Blackpool's heritage and cultural landscape. It also articulated a desire to establish a national seaside centre, but perhaps most audaciously it recommended that Blackpool should seek to be inscribed as a World Heritage Site. Its submission to be placed on the United Kingdom's Tentative List explained Blackpool's role in the development of a form of mass tourism in Britain that was exported to the world, and described how the

Figure 103
*Such a striking lighting scheme may not seem
an obvious solution for dealing with a street in a
conservation area, but it reflects Blackpool's long
tradition of seeking novel, high-quality ways to
appeal to visitors.*
[DP154803]

existing town and its buildings illustrated the development of seaside holidays. However, in March 2011 the Independent Expert Panel Report to the Department for Culture, Media and Sport rejected Blackpool's inclusion on the list.

In 2010 Blackpool Council set out again its vision for the town centre and summarised what had been achieved already in trying to create 'The City on the Beach':

> The Tower, Piers, Winter Gardens, Pleasure Beach and Tramway are revitalised, complemented by new events and attractions. Pedestrian friendly regenerated streets and new public squares accommodate a Blackpool café culture, with attractive and enjoyable public realm throughout the centre, reconnecting the town to the sea. There are new hotels and new aspirational housing, and the town centre and resort are easy to get to and move around in.[50]

Nevertheless, the strategy recognised there was still a need to strengthen the town centre's identity and economy by improving the retail offer, enhancing existing attractions and providing new reasons to visit. The Winter Gardens was recognised as a separate quarter and the report recommended that proposals should be developed for mixed retail, leisure and conference facilities, including a hotel and complementary parking spaces. The Winter Gardens and the Tower were bought by Blackpool Council in 2010 and ambitious restoration programmes for both have begun to revive these key attractions (Fig 104). English Heritage and Blackpool Council have funded Conservation Management Plans for both sites to help to recognise how future development can be achieved while maintaining the historic character of the structures. In 2012 Blackpool Council decided that the management of the Winter Gardens should be put out to tender and the successful bidder would identify how to manage and adapt the site to meet the market requirements of its customers. Blackpool Tower is now managed by the Merlin Entertainment Group, and a new Dungeon attraction and improved observation deck have already been completed.

Figure 104
The Floral Hall was a key part of the original Winter Gardens that opened in 1878. This central circulation space has been the subject of a high-quality restoration programme by the council since 2010.
[DP117483]

Blackpool in the future

Blackpool has faced significant economic and social challenges since the mid-20th century and these are still obvious in parts of the town. In the 2010 Index of Multiple Deprivation, Blackpool came 10th out 326 local authorities, but this is because the town's more affluent residential areas prevented it from achieving an even higher position in the league table. When Blackpool is broken down into Lower Layer Super Output Areas the level of deprivation in its central areas is more obvious. England is divided into over 32,000 of these units, but Blackpool has 3 in the top 10 most deprived list and 12 in the top 100. Nevertheless there appear to be some reasons for optimism. Since 1991 the town's population has risen by about 4,000 and visitor numbers appear to be rising, with 13 million people apparently visiting in 2010. Tourism remains a huge industry in England and Wales, directly employing 210,000 people, almost as many as are involved in the telecommunications industry and more than in the motor industry. In 2009 a report for Blackpool Council suggested that almost 25,000 jobs were dependent on the holiday trade and tourism expenditure was over £1 billion, while another study in 2010 suggested that almost 20,000 jobs in the Greater Blackpool area were derived from tourism.

A decade after the Masterplan was adopted in Blackpool it is clear that much has been achieved to implement its vision. The arrival experience for motorists leaving the M55 has been improved, a new, modern tramway system has been installed and the central promenade and its sea defences have been transformed. In the town centre significant public-realm improvements have also taken place, many buildings are in a better state of repair and the stirrings of a new café culture can already be witnessed. The redevelopment of the Talbot Gateway is underway and Blackpool's key buildings, the Tower and the Winter Gardens, are being restored, though there are many challenges that lie ahead.

When Pevsner wrote about Blackpool in 1969 he found that it had no listed buildings, but by the mid-1970s the Grand Theatre (1972), the Tower and the Winter Gardens (1973), Clifton Hotel and Town Hall (1974) and the North Pier (1975) were listed. Today the local authority has 41 designated buildings and structures, though fewer than half are directly related to the town's seaside heritage. Most recently the Savoy Garage has been added to this list as a result of thematic work being carried out by English Heritage into the impact of the car on the built environment (Fig 105). Relatively few of Blackpool's buildings are eligible for designation by the Department for Culture, Media and Sport as it was a town that had largely developed after 1850 and its buildings have been regularly adapted to meet the changing expectations of customers, as well as dealing with the ravages of a seafront location. This does not mean that Blackpool does not have a rich seaside heritage. To identify and characterise the key areas of Blackpool, English Heritage helped to fund six historic townscape characterisation studies carried out for Blackpool Council by Architectural History Practice. The project examined historic buildings in the study areas and assigned significance to each building, a process that will lead to the best examples being considered for a new local list. The council's approach to regeneration, working on Blackpool's distinctive neighbourhoods,

Figure 105
The Savoy Garage was built in 1914–15, probably by T G Lumb, Son & Walton of Blackpool. It was originally built to serve the nearby Savoy Hotel, which opened in 1915.
[AA053225]

could provide a framework for the creation of new conservation areas in the future that would help to improve the built environment and celebrate the town's special character.

Blackpool faces the challenge of providing jobs, homes and services for its residents while retaining the loyalty of its existing visitors and reaching out to new markets. To attract new customers it has recognised the need to improve what it already offers without alienating its traditional market, but a new, younger, more affluent visitor will want modern entertainments, state-of-the-art facilities and comfortable accommodation. The revived central promenade

Figure 106
Gigantic dune grass sculptures sway gently in the wind in front of entertainment complexes in the centre of the Golden Mile, and no postcard view is ever complete without the Tower, the symbol of Blackpool and the British seaside.
[DP154758]

typifies this challenge; there is a need to retain a traditional promenade and a well-loved tram system for its regular visitors, while meeting the needs of the town's residents and protecting the town centre. However, Blackpool Council has imaginatively bound new attractions into the scheme; a paving scheme based on a century of comedy and 30m-high dune grass would not seem to be the obvious solution to improving the public realm in most historic towns, but perfectly embody Blackpool's heritage and its history of looking forward at the same time as cherishing its colourful past (Fig 106).

Notes

1 Luke 1919, 273; Priestley 1934, 263

2 Granville 1841, 347

3 Cartwright 1889, 6

4 Baines 1824, 526

5 Hutton 1891, 56

6 Whittle 1831, 7–8

7 Hutton 1789, 28, 5

8 Ayton 1815, 102

9 Ayton 1815, 103

10 Thornber 1837, 223–224n

11 Hutton 1891, 56; Ayton 1815, 103

12 The *General Evening Post* (London) 19–21 June 1792. Extract in *St Annes Express* 24 August 1910, in Blackpool Local and Family History Centre M851 (p) C R 17 971

13 Porter 1876, 312–3

14 Hutton 1789, 28; Chester Record Office DFF/34/51, 13 Oct 1789

15 Thornber 1837, 73

16 Thornber 1837, 289

17 *Preston Chronicle and Lancashire Advertiser* 23 May 1863, 7

18 Baines 1836, 425–6

19 Hutton 1789, 42

20 Hutton 1789, 52

21 Cheshire Record Office DFF/34/51

22 Hutton 1789, 28

23 Whittle 1831, 14

24 Hutton 1789, 31

25 Hutton 1789, 37

26 Thornber 1837, 226

27 Granville 1841, 347

28 Whittle 1831, 17

29 Baines 1824, 528; Thornber 1837, 234

30 Thornber 1837, 237

31 Thornber 1837, 239

32 Granville 1841, 350

33 Slater 1848, 298

34 Porter 1866, 27

35 Porter 1866, 20

36 Blackpool *Gazette and News* 30 May 1873, 1

37 Blackpool Corporation 1897, advertisement

38 Blackpool *Gazette and News* 16 April 1897, 8

39 Blackpool *Gazette and News* 27 July 1894, 6

40 Anon 1895, unpaginated

41 Anon 1899, 18; Blackpool *Gazette and News* 12 May 1899, 1

42 Blackpool Corporation 1897, 23

43 Blackpool Corporation 1889, xv, advertisement

44 Blackpool *Gazette and News* 29 July 1904, 8

45 Mawson 1927, 340–2

46 Jones 1939, 2

47 Robinson 1939

48 Pevsner 1969, 68

49 English Heritage Urban Panel 2003

50 Blackpool Council 2010, 8

References and selected further reading

Anon 1895 *Illustrated Guide to the Blackpool Tower, and Programme of Amusements*

Anon 1899 *The Alhambra, Blackpool*. Blackpool

Anon 1939 'New Casino, Blackpool'. *Architects' Journal* **90**, 27 July 1939, 133–8

Ayton, Richard 1815 *A Voyage Round Great Britain Undertaken in the Summer of the Year 1813*. Vol 1 of 8 vols, London: Longman

Baines, Edward 1824 *History, Directory, and Gazetteer of the County Palatine of Lancaster*. 2 vols, Liverpool: William Wales

Baines, Edward 1836 *History of the County Palatine and Duchy of Lancaster*. Vol 4 of 4 vols, London: Fisher, Son and Co

Bairstow, Martin 2001 *Railways of Blackpool and the Fylde*. Martin Bairstow

Blackpool Corporation 1889 *The Popular Guide to Blackpool*. Blackpool

Blackpool Corporation 1897 *Blackpool, The Unrivalled Seaside Resort for Health and Leisure*. Blackpool

Blackpool Corporation 1926 *Blackpool's Progress*. Blackpool

Blackpool Council 2010 *Blackpool Town Centre Strategy Draft for Consultation*. http://www.blackpool.gov.uk/NR/rdonlyres/968A40B9-6050-49A0-BD44-53B264434B3C/0/BLACKPOOLTOWNCENTRESTRATEGY100517small.pdf [accessed 27 February 2013]

British Film Institute, 2005 *Electric Edwardians*. DVD

Brodie, Allan and Winter, Gary 2007 *The English Seaside Resort*. Swindon: English Heritage

Cartwright, James Joel (ed) 1889 *The Travels through England of Dr Richard Pococke*. Vol 2, London: Camden Society

Clarke, Allen 1923 *The Story of Blackpool*. Blackpool: Palatine Books

Curtis, Bill 1988 *Blackpool Tower*. Lavenham: Terence Dalton

English Heritage Urban Panel 2003 *Review of the Panel's Visit to Blackpool with Representatives of CABE on 27/28 January 2003*

Granville, Augustus Bozzi 1841 *The Spas of England and Principal Sea-bathing Places, Northern Spas*. London

Hartwell, Clare and Pevsner, Nikolaus 2009 *Lancashire: North*. London: Yale University Press

Hutton, William 1789 *A Description of Blackpool in Lancashire; Frequented for Sea Bathing*. Birmingham: Pearson and Rollason

Hutton, Catherine 1891 *Reminiscences of a Gentlewoman of the Last Century: Letters of Catherine Hutton*. Birmingham: Cornish Brothers

Jones, Trevor T 1939 'Blackpool's Success?' Supplement to *Blackpool Herald and Gazette*, 6 May 1939, 2

Lightbown, Ted 1994 *Blackpool: A Pictorial History*. Chichester: Phillimore

Luke, T D 1919 *Spas and Health Resorts of the British Isles*. London: A&C Black

Mawson, Thomas H 1927 *The Life & Work of an English Landscape Architect: An Autobiography by Thomas H Mawson*, London: Richards Press

Morrison, Kathryn A and Minnis, John 2012 *Carscapes: The Motor Car, Landscape and Architecture in England*. London: Yale University Press

Palmer, Steve 2012 *New Trams to the Tower*. Fleetwood: Hesketh Press

Pevsner, Nikolaus 1969 *The Buildings of England: Lancashire (the Rural North)*. London: Penguin Books

Porter, John 1876 *History of the Fylde of Lancashire*. Fleetwood and Blackpool: W Porter and Sons

Porter, W 1866 *Porter's Guidebook to Blackpool*. Blackpool and Fleetwood: W Porter

Priestley, J B 1934 *English Journey*. London: William Heinemann

Robinson, J C 1939 'Building for the Future', Supplement to *Blackpool Herald and Gazette*, 6 May 1939

Slater, 1848 *Directory of Lancashire*. Manchester: Slater

Smith, Janet 2005 *Liquid Assets: The Lidos and Open Air Swimming Pools of Britain*. London: English Heritage

Thornber, William 1837 *An Historical and Descriptive Account of Blackpool*. Poulton: William Thornber

Toulmin, Vanessa 2009 *Winter Gardens Blackpool: The Most Magnificent Palace of Amusement in the World*. Hathersage: Boco Publishing

Toulmin, Vanessa 2011 *Blackpool Pleasure Beach: More Than Just an Amusement Park*. Hathersage: Boco Publishing

Toulmin, Vanessa 2011 *Blackpool Tower: Wonderland of the World*. Hathersage: Boco Publishing

Toulmin, Vanessa 2012 *Blackpool Illuminations: The Greatest Free Show on Earth*. Hathersage: Boco Publishing

Walton, John K 1974 'The social development of Blackpool, 1788–1914'. Ph.D. thesis, Lancaster University

Walton, John K 1983 *The English Seaside Resort: A Social History, 1750–1914*. Leicester: Leicester University Press

Walton, John K 1994 'The re-making of a popular resort: Blackpool Tower and the boom of the 1890s'. *The Local Historian*, November 1994

Walton, John K 1998 *Blackpool*. Edinburgh: Edinburgh University Press; Lancaster: Carnegie Publishing

Walton, John K 2000 *The British Seaside: Holidays and Resorts in the Twentieth Century*. Manchester: Manchester University Press

Walton, John K 2007 *Riding on Rainbows: Blackpool Pleasure Beach and its Place in British Popular Culture*. St Albans: Skelter Publishing

Whittle, Peter 1831 *Marina*. Preston: P&H Whittle

Wood, Alan and Lightbown, Ted 2010 *Blackpool Through Time*. Stroud: Amberley Books

Woodman, John 2011 *Municipal Transport in Transition*. Blackpool: Rigby Road Publishing

Other titles in the Informed Conservation series

Alston Moor: Buildings in a North Pennines landscape.
Lucy Jessop and Matthew Whitfield, with Andrew Davison, 2013.
Product code 51755, ISBN 9781848021174

Ancoats: Cradle of industrialisation.
Michael E Rose with Keith Falconer and Julian Holder, 2011.
Product code 51453, ISBN 9781848020276

Berwick-upon-Tweed: Three places, two nations, one town.
Adam Menuge with Catherine Dewar, 2009.
Product code 51471, ISBN 9781848020290

Building a Better Society: Liverpool's historic institutional buildings.
Colum Giles, 2008.
Product code 51332, ISBN 9781873592908

Built on Commerce: Liverpool's central business district.
Joseph Sharples and John Stonard, 2008.
Product code 51331, ISBN 9781905624348

Defending Scilly.
Mark Bowden and Allan Brodie, 2011.
Product code 51530, ISBN 9781848020436

England's Schools: History, architecture and adaptation.
Elain Harwood, 2010.
Product code 51476, ISBN 9781848020313

English Garden Cities: An introduction.
Mervyn Miller, 2010.
Product code 51532, ISBN 9781848020511

The Hat Industry of Luton and its Buildings.
Katie Carmichael, David McOmish and David Grech, 2013.
Product code 51750, ISBN 9781848021198

Manchester's Northern Quarter.
Simon Taylor and Julian Holder, 2008.
Product code 50946, ISBN 9781873592847

Manchester: The warehouse legacy – An introduction and guide.
Simon Taylor, Malcolm Cooper and P S Barnwell, 2002.
Product code 50668, ISBN 9781873592670

Manningham: Character and diversity in a Bradford suburb.
Simon Taylor and Kathryn Gibson, 2010.
Product code 51475, ISBN 9781848020306

Margate's Seaside Heritage.
Nigel Barker, Allan Brodie, Nick Dermott, Lucy Jessop and Gary Winter, 2007.
Product code 51335, ISBN 9781905624669

Ordinary Landscapes, Special Places: Anfield, Breckfield and the growth of Liverpool's suburbs.
Adam Menuge, 2008.
Product code 51343, ISBN 9781873592892

Places of Health and Amusement: Liverpool's historic parks and gardens.
Katy Layton-Jones and Robert Lee, 2008.
Product code 51333, ISBN 9781873592915

Religion and Place in Leeds.
John Minnis with Trevor Mitchell, 2007.
Product code 51337, ISBN 9781905624485

Stourport-on-Severn: Pioneer town of the canal age.
Colum Giles, Keith Falconer, Barry Jones and Michael Taylor, 2007.
Product code 51290, ISBN 9781905624362

Weymouth's Seaside Heritage.
Allan Brodie, Colin Ellis, David Stuart and Gary Winter, 2008.
Product code 51429, ISBN 9781848020085

Further information on titles in the Informed Conservation series can be found on our website.

To order through EH Sales
Tel: 01235 465577
Fax: 01235 465556
Email: direct.orders@marston.co.uk

Online bookshop: www.english-heritageshop.org.uk

Gazetteer

North Blackpool

1 Cliffs Hotel, Queen's Promenade

Built in 1921, the hotel was extended in 1936–7 by Halstead Best, who doubled the accommodation, incorporated an underground car park and added a large central tower.

2 Pulhamite cliffs and seafront gardens, Queen's Promenade

A short stretch of sunken ornamental gardens was completed in 1915, and this was followed in 1923 by a stretch of landscaping that created natural-looking cliffs made out of Pulhamite, an artificial rock.

3 Savoy Hotel, Queen's Promenade

The hotel, which opened in 1915 and originally had 300 rooms, was designed by local architect by Tom G Lumb. A very early, purpose-built garage for guests opened in 1915 in King George Avenue to the north of the hotel.

4 The Gynn Inn

A modern traffic roundabout marks the site of the 18th-century inn, which closed in 1921. The present Gynn public house was built in 1939 by Halstead Best on the site of the Duke of Cambridge Hotel, which had been built in the 1860s.

5 Site of the Derby Baths, Promenade

The baths were designed by J C Robinson and opened in 1939. After a major extension they were officially reopened in 1965. They were closed and demolished in 1990.

6 Sea defences and colonnades

The Princess Parade Colonnade, stretching northwards from the Metropole, was designed by the Borough Surveyor J S Brodie and opened in 1912. The Middle Walk Colonnade further to the north was built in 1923–5 by J C Robinson.

7 Imperial Hotel, Promenade

The Imperial Hotel, built in 1866–7 by Clegg and Knowles, was extended by Mangnall and Littlewood in the mid-1870s. In 1904 a substantial extension was added to the north side by J D Broadbent.

8 Site of seawater pumping station, Dickson Road

In 1872 the Blackpool Sea Water Company was established to supply seawater. The pumping station designed by Garlick, Park and Sykes opened in 1873, but unfortunately it was destroyed by fire in 2006.

9 Lansdowne Crescent, Promenade

Lansdowne Crescent was built from 1864. It was the earliest example of a four-storeyed structure on the seafront, predating the Clifton Arms Hotel and the Imperial Hotel.

10 Imperial Picture Palace, Dickson Road

This cinema, which opened on 14 July 1913, was refurbished after a fire in 1939 but closed in 1961. It is now used as an advice centre.

11 Site of swimming baths, Cocker Street

The baths were built in 1870 and refitted in 1873. They were purchased by Blackpool Corporation in 1905 and demolished in March 1974, leaving the site as a car park.

12 Regent Court, Promenade

This 1960s residential block of flats is notable in Blackpool for its rarity. Tall towers are features of many seafronts, particularly in south-east England, but it is unusual to find one so close to the heart of the historic town.

The Gynn sign [AA060381]

King Edward Avenue
Queen's Promenade
Warbreck Hill Road
Gynn Sq
Devonshire Road
Warley Road
Carshalton Road
Claremont Road
Leaysley Road
Fielding Road
Derby Road
Clevedon Road
Chesterfield Road
Egerton Road
Cheltenham Road
Enfield Road
Hawthorn Road
Dickson Road
Clifford Road
Pleasant Street
Talbot Road
Promenade
Cocker Street
High Street
Lord Street
General Street
Station

0   100   500 metres

Central Blackpool

13 Former Odeon Cinema, Dickson Road

Opened in 1939, the auditorium contained more than 3,000 seats. The architect was Robert Bullivant of Harry Weedon and Partners, the firm responsible for the Odeon chain's major 1930s push for expansion.

14 Metropole Hotel, Promenade

By the 1780s Bailey's Hotel was one of the handful of large houses providing guests with accommodation. The hotel was enlarged and rebuilt during the 19th century and underwent a lavish refurbishment and extension before reopening in 1900.

15 Former Princess Cinema, Promenade

Originally opened in 1912, the cinema was significantly enlarged and reopened in 1922. The cinema continued in use until 1981 and is now a nightclub.

16 Central Library and Grundy Art Gallery, Queen Street

The library and art gallery opened in 1911 following a bequest of 33 artworks and a financial gift from John and Cuthbert Grundy. The building was designed by Cullen, Lochhead and Brown in an Edwardian Baroque style.

17 Former site of Talbot Road Station

The original railway station, a large classical building, opened in 1846 on a site nearer the centre of town than the modern station. It was rebuilt in 1896–8 and demolished to make way for a supermarket that opened in 1979.

18 Car park and bus station, Talbot Road

Opened in 1939, this multi-storey car park was the first such facility in the country built by a local authority, and one of the earliest multi-storey car parks outside London.

19 Roman Catholic church, Talbot Road

The original church was built in 1857 by E W Pugin and the nave and aisles survive from this phase. The east end was rebuilt in 1894 by Pugin and Pugin.

20 North Pier

Blackpool's first pier, which opened in 1863, was designed by the leading pier engineer Eugenius Birch. Its pierhead was enlarged to house the Indian Pavilion of 1877 and the pier was doubled in width in 1897.

21 Clifton (Arms) Hotel, Talbot Square

Originally a small Georgian hotel, the eastern half of the current structure was erected in the mid-1860s while the western half, where the Georgian hotel had survived, was rebuilt a decade later.

22 Town Hall, Talbot Square

The original building of 1900 was designed by Potts, Son and Hennings in a Jacobean style. The extension at the rear was built in 1937–8 by J C Robinson. On its exterior there is a frieze of panels depicting forms of transport.

23 Site of Theatre Royal, Arcade and Assembly Room, Talbot Square

This large, four-storeyed building was designed by Speakman and Charlesworth and opened in 1868. A library was

North Pier [AA060376]

established there in 1880 and in 1896 it was taken over by Yates's. A fire in 2009 completely destroyed the building.

24 Roberts' Oyster Bar, Promenade

This three-storeyed, mid-19th-century house is a rare survivor from early Blackpool. The prominent signs were probably added in or after the 1870s when the building was taken over by Roberts to be used as an oyster bar.

25 Birley Street

This street was laid out in the 1840s as part of the development of land owned by Thomas Clifton and the trustees of the Lytham School. It is now dominated by a modern disco lighting scheme set in large arches that span the street.

26 St John's Church, Church Street

A new parish church was built in 1878 by Garlick, Park and Sykes, replacing the earlier church of 1821. The church was subdivided in 2005 to provide a small place of worship as well as a heritage centre and café.

27 Savoy Café, Promenade

Opened in 1938 and designed by Derham, MacKeith and Partners, the café was one of the few buildings along the promenade that employed a modernist style, with long ranges of horizontal windows and clean lines.

28 Grand Theatre, Church Street

'Matcham's Masterpiece', which opened in 1894, was designed by the renowned theatre architect Frank Matcham. It has

Winter Gardens [DP154990]

a flamboyant free Baroque exterior and lavish interiors.

29 Winter Gardens

The Winter Gardens opened in 1878, and in the following half-century a series of large venues was added, including the Empress Ballroom (1896), Olympia (1930), several themed rooms (1931) and the third Opera House (1939).

30 Raikes Hall, Liverpool Road

The gardens of this mid-18th-century house became pleasure gardens in 1872. By 1901 it had closed and the site was redeveloped for housing.

31 Site of the Alhambra

In the 1830s Hygiene Terrace was built on this site. It was replaced by the Prince of Wales Theatre (1877) and adjacent baths (1881). These were demolished to make way for the Alhambra, which opened in 1899. It was replaced in 1964 by Lewis' Department Store, which closed in 1993. The site is now occupied by a former Woolworths store and other shops.

32 Site of Victoria Promenade, Victoria Street

In 1837 a small, purpose-built assembly room above shops was built. It is now the site of a shop that opened in 2000. In 1933 the Little Vic pub, with an oriental-inspired façade, opened at the eastern end of the assembly room.

33 Comedy Carpet and Festival House, Promenade

The Comedy Carpet and Festival House are part of the major promenade improvements that were completed in 2012.

34 Blackpool Tower

Sir Benjamin Heywood's house, which was built in 1837, became an aquarium that opened in 1875. In 1894 the Tower opened on this site.

Grand Theatre [DP033750]

35 Former Woolworths Building and site of Palatine Hotel

Completed in 1938 by the company architect William Priddle, this was one of the largest stores in the Woolworths empire.

36 Lockhart's Café, Bank Hey Street/ Adelaide Street East

Another large café building by Derham, MacKeith and Partners in a modern style, it was completed in 1937 on one of the main shopping streets of the town.

37 Central Station

This station opened in 1863. It was rebuilt in 1899–1901 but closed in 1964, and the site is now a car park. The site was earmarked for the proposed regional casino.

38 Central Picture Theatre, Central Drive

This cinema, which dates from 1913, became the King Edward Cinema. It was later used as a bingo hall and then as a nightclub.

39 Law Courts and Police Station, Chapel Street

Built on the site of the infamous Bonny's Estate, these brutalist buildings, which opened in 1971, were constructed on top of a podium with car parking below.

40 Villas on Chapel Street and Bethesda

This is a small enclave of Gothic-style villas, the earliest of which dates from c 1870. Their location beside the railway line seems to be at odds with their relatively high status.

41 Central Pier

Blackpool's second pier was designed by John Isaac Mawson and was officially opened on 30 May 1868. A popular venue for outdoor dancing, it was aimed at a more popular market than the North Pier.

42 Foxhall, Promenade

Now the site of a modern pub, Foxhall was originally the seat of the Tyldesley family and seems to have been built in the 17th century. It was one of the houses that provided accommodation for the earliest visitors.

43 Original tramway depot and gasworks

This area beside the railway line into Central Station became the location for the town's early gasworks, tram depot and electric power station.

44 Tyldesley Terrace, Promenade

This terrace of 1880 is one of the earliest examples of substantial four-storeyed houses on the seafront.

45 Royal Pavilion Cinema, Rigby Road

This is the earliest surviving cinema in Blackpool. It opened in 1909 as the home for A1 Animated Pictures, which used to be in the nearby Colosseum.

46 Manchester Hotel, Promenade/ Lytham Road

The original 1845 building was replaced in 1936 by J C Derham, who employed an opulent Moderne style in his design. The building was completely rebuilt in 1996.

47 Lifeboat station, Lytham Road

In 1864 the first purpose-built lifeboat station was erected. A new lifeboat station by Halstead Best opened in 1937 beside Central Pier, but this was demolished when the new sea defences were created.

48 Tram depot and Blackpool Transport offices, Blundell Street

The large depot, which opened in 1935, provided accommodation for the Corporation's expanded fleet of trams. A new office building was erected alongside in 1937–8 to designs by Halstead Best.

Central Picture Theatre [DP155000]